Serfing America

The Progressive Destruction of the American Dream

SUE ANN THIELKE

ROGER BALL

All Bible quotes are from the NIV through the on line pastor resource
https://www.wordsearchbible.com/ws10

Cover photo: inhauscreative/IStock
"Destroying the Bill of Rights"

Contact us on Facebook - Serfing America
or
https://www.facebook.com/pages/Serfing-America/812895688767071

ISBN: 1502777495
ISBN 13: 9781502777492

To a Free and Sovereign America

It does not take a majority to prevail...
but rather an irate, tireless minority,
keen on setting brushfires of freedom in the minds of men.

Samuel Adams[1]

ACKNOWLEDGMENTS

We were carried along the way and wish to thank…

Pastor James Perry for mentoring us through a very long process. James is an encourager and a gentleman.

Mary Ridlon Ph.D. for patiently editing two novice writers' manuscripts with a spirit of professionalism, generosity and patience. Mary's double Ph.D. is evident in her editing.

Ann Kentees and Mark Thielke for their TLC in more ways than we can count.

Craig McGarvey Ed.D., and Diane Singer for encouragement and editing wisdom.

Laura Ball for graciously pitching in to free up Roger for this endeavor.

We have done our best to footnote and give credit where it is due. If a mistake was made or a credit omitted we are profoundly sorry. Many of the cultural examples we used are cited with links which may become hard to locate over time. A few of the examples we cited, partially legal cases, may have changed or been reversed.

Special thanks to Dinesh D'Souza for writing his inspiring book *America: Imagine a World without Her* and the late F.A. Hayek for his classic *The Road to Serfdom*.

TABLE OF CONTENTS

INTRODUCTION

We titled our book *Serfing America* because "serfing" is precisely what the Progressives are doing to the middle class. A serf is a worker who is allowed to keep some of the fruits of his labor. A serf was far worse off than our Founders' vision of a laissez-faire worker in America. Laissez-faire is "a doctrine opposing governmental interference in economic affairs beyond the minimum necessary for the maintenance of peace and property rights."[2]

Karl Marx points out that "the peasant serf…worked three days for himself on his own field or the field allotted to him, and the three subsequent days he performed compulsory and gratuitous labor on the estate of his lord." Marx appreciated the clarity of the system: "here the paid and unpaid part of labor were sensibly separated." So at least the serf could realize the degree to which he was being ripped off. And the thieves were the lords and aristocrats, who lived off the labor of the serfs. The serf worked, and they ate.

America's tax rates, we may recall with some surprise, impose basically the same terms on successful citizens as those imposed on the medieval serf. The top federal rate is nearly 40 percent, and with other taxes piled on, the top rate easily reaches 50 percent. What this means is that half of the labor of these citizens is confiscated up front; another way to look at it is that the first half of the year they work for the government, and only the second half of the year they work for themselves and their families.[3]

America's tax rates impose basically the same terms on successful citizens as those imposed on the medieval serf. The Progressive attack is multifaceted and seeks to destroy our Founders brilliant work in a myriad of ways.

How can it be that the America in which I grew up is imploding before my eyes? The impact of the Progressive Movement tsunami of reforms is stunning as it seeps into every nook and cranny of our culture. How can it be that a majority of the American people, including many Christians, would freely choose to embrace secular values rather than those of the Judeo-Christian worldview? I asked myself, why is it many of our leaders are employing every tactic at their disposal, some legal and some illegal, to unravel the founding principles that made America great? Why are the Liberals intentionally attacking excellence and all that is holy and good? Or put another way, why do they embrace mediocrity and often glorify the violent, hateful and vulgar?

I believe ideas are being implanted in our youth that are treasonous and will undertake to prove it in this book.

> Millions of parents are sending their kids to public schools without having any idea that they are being taught that **patriotism** is divisive, that **capitalism** is evil and that **Christianity** is a fictitious cult. Instead of learning traditional American values, those kids are being taught that they should identify themselves as "global citizens", that socialism is about "sharing" and that all of the religions of the world need to come together as one.[4]

The Progressive dream is to help our own and others through the "fair" distribution of assets. Our Framers' American dream has always been to help our own and others to be all they can be through hard work and innovation.

How can it be that the clash of these two schools of thought has created such hatred and gridlock of ideas? Progressives like Barack Obama and Hilary Clinton are repackaged liberals. The term "Progressive" is nothing more and nothing less than a facelift for the old worn out "liberal" or "socialist" school of thought. To put it simply, it's the big government types attempting to rejuvenate their brand as they march forward. Progressives, like President Obama and Hillary Clinton, are one world utopists. They work hard and dream of a planet without national boundaries, with one centralized all powerful government which spreads the wealth evenly around like mayonnaise on a BLT. Can any smart minded person imagine anyone contemplating to deal fairly with the Taliban, al-Qaida, or ISIS-Islamic State in Syria-to name a few.

Progressives are working hard to share America's wealth as atonement for past sins they believe America committed and continues to commit. They strive to make reparations for past injustices in the world using our tax dollars. These repackaged liberals assume the only thing that made America great was little more than the plunder of goods and services. Dinesh D'Souza explains they fail to realize that:

> America is founded on the understanding that wealth can be created through innovation and enterprise. Through the system of technological capitalism, we can go from ten marbles to twenty marbles without taking anyone's marbles. Obviously there were inventors and merchants around before America. But America is the first society to be based on invention and trade. America is the capitalist society par excellence.[5]

This book is about the Progressives' deliberate attack on Patriotism, Capitalism and the Judeo-Christian worldview.

Tragically, most of America is clueless as to the magnitude of the attacks. Our Founder's vision has been cast aside in favor of the orthodoxy of secularism, America's majority religion espousing the altar call, "It's all about me." Promoting secularism is a favorite propaganda tool of the Progressives.

Sadly, we must understand one thing from the get-go: America is now post Christian in its worldview. To call America post Christian is heart wrenching. This book was originally intended to be a warning about the many ways our government and its liberal allies, such as Hollywood and the media elite, are joining forces to eliminate God from every facet of our lives. Through my research I have come to realize Progressive attacks on God are part of a bigger plan that involves the taking down of not only Christianity but Capitalism and American truths as well. They have a well-laid-out plan of attack neatly packaged as a college textbook titled *Rules for Radicals* by Saul Alinsky.

I became a Cultural Warrior under the mentoring of the late Charles Colson (Breakpoint). His "The Centurion Program" first planted in me the seed to write a book about America's cultural decline. Chuck's vision was for Centurions to become modern day prophets proclaiming to the culture at large and the church that things are not right and we must return to the Judeo-Christian worldview. Pastor Roger Ball, of Freedom Church in Vero Beach, Florida, accepted my offer to co-author. Roger comes to the pulpit from a business background and is the perfect partner for a project such as this. Week after week, Roger's sermons remind me of Charles Colson. Roger will address Saul Alinsky's rules and explain how devastating they are to the American Dream later in our book.

PART I

THE PROGRESSIVE ATTACK ON PATRIOTISM

1

THE AMERICAN EXPERIMENT

Memorial Day and the Fourth of July were intended to be reverent holidays, days set aside to express profound respect, not just days off from work to celebrate backyard barbeque feasts, or heading to the beach or lake bearing coolers overflowing with beer and soda. They were national holidays specifically set aside to honor and celebrate the many sacrifices made by our men and women serving in the armed forces, past and present. Everyone set time aside to honor our Founding Fathers for tirelessly birthing our glorious Republic. We were taught, at home and at school, to not only respect but pay tribute to America's Framers, national treasures who wrote the Constitution and other documents interwoven together to form our wonderful experiment. Americans were proud of all we call America every day, but especially on Memorial Day and the Fourth of July. We proudly displayed the Red, White and Blue and felt inspired to be born in the U.S.A.

Today many within the Progressive Movement resent the observance of our national holidays. Dinesh D'Souza puts it succinctly,

> Both sides love America, but they love a different type of America. One side loves the America of Columbus and the Fourth of July, of

3

innovation and work and the "animal spirit" of capitalism, of the Boy Scouts and parochial schools, of traditional families and flag-saluting veterans. The other side loves the America of tolerance and social entitlements, of income and wealth redistribution, of affirmative action and abortion, of feminism and gay marriage.[6]

When Columbus ran ashore in America in 1492, I am sure that no one was more surprised than he was.

His voyages led to the first lasting European contact with the Americas, inaugurating a period of European exploration, conquest, and colonization that lasted for several centuries. They had, therefore, an enormous impact in the historical development of the modern Western world. Columbus himself saw his accomplishments primarily in the light of spreading the Christian religion.[7]

When we read Columbus's diaries we see that his motives are complex: he wanted to get rich by discovering new trade routes, but he also wanted to find the Garden of Eden, which he believed was an actual undiscovered place. Of course, Columbus didn't come looking for America; he didn't know that the American continent existed. Since the Muslims controlled the trade routes to the Arabian Sea, he was looking for a new way to the Far East. Specifically he was looking for India, and that's why he called the native peoples "Indians." It is easy to laugh at Columbus's naïveté, except that he was not entirely wrong. Anthropological research has established that the native people of the Americas did originally come from Asia. Most likely they came across the Bering Strait before the continents drifted apart.[8]

Columbus was the first to bring the Judeo-Christian worldview to America. The subjects of the King that arrived on our shores in 1620 were fleeing state persecution. They were brave resourceful and enterprising. They came prepared to work the land and make a new life for themselves. They believed they were providentially sent to America to colonize one nation under God. I have visited the Pilgrims' traditional arrival site, Plymouth Rock, and although it is not much to look at, it brings awe, sacrifice and thankfulness to mind. You know, 1620 was not all that long ago! Columbus was the first to bring the Biblical worldview to our shores but as early as 1607 Jamestown was founded for the sake of mining gold.

Our Founders, without exception, believed Judeo-Christian values were necessary if the country were to prosper. As Benjamin Franklin put it, "Only a virtuous people are capable of freedom. As nations become corrupt and vicious, they have more need of masters."[9] Our Founders realized that since day one, man has sought to make things better and more comfortable for himself. The worldview of our Founders tells us that Adam and Eve were the first humans to attempt to rewrite the rules as they gorged on forbidden fruit. The world turned upside down, *everything changed,* because the one rule God asked Adam and Eve to adhere to did not seem fair to them. They wanted life in the garden to be on their terms, certainly NOT God's! Adam and Eve were, from their perspective, victims. They wanted their "fair share." Eve cried, "The devil made me do it!" Adam blamed Eve and the blame game of victimization began. Since that fateful day, man continues to look at himself as a victim. Adam and Eve knew better. Adam and Eve laid the foundation for today's "it's all about me" culture. If we are honest with one another, and you and I were to swap places with Adam and Eve, I am sure we would succumb to the enticements or lure of the world as well. We, like our ancestors in the garden, are turning our back on God. We are no smarter than Adam and Eve. We just have more tools.

Anne Graham Lotz put it very well on September 11, 2001, after the terrorist attacks took place.

> For several years now Americans in a sense have shaken their fist at God and said, "God, we want you out of our schools, government, our businesses; we want you out of our marketplace." And, God, who is a gentleman, has just quietly backed out of our national and political life, our public life, removing His hand of blessing and protection.[10]

Our Founders envisioned that their job or goal was to design a form of government which would maintain security, justice and good order, taking into account the history of other governments and the inclinations of man. It was no easy feat engineering a system of government that sought to control a propensity for self-destruction which is part of human nature. What our Founders came up with was truly miraculous. The United States was the first to build a government around natural law and a free-market. Many call our country "The American Experiment," which should remind every American that many experiments fail even after starting out to be remarkably successful. To name a few of the more iconic, recall the RMS Titanic, Apple's Lisa, the Ford Edsel, the New Coke, the Tower of Pisa, Chernobyl, and the Challenger lift off. "In 1776, 98 percent of the people in America professed to be Protestant Christians."[11] Foundational to the American Experiment is the fact that in seventeenth century England, Christians fleeing religious persecution, founded the nation. It makes sense then that the American experiment is an outgrowth of how they envisioned the world around them. Every one of the early settlements was made up of Christians from one denomination or another, but credit goes to the Puritans for casting the vision of a government based on the Judeo-Christian worldview. We consider it innovative, but it seemed like common sense to them. They were brilliant men using Puritan church covenants and the Bible as templates to seed the land we call America.

Incredibly, our Founders did not feel the need to write a book of laws. They believed that laws or rules came naturally to man. They had no doubt that the knowledge of right and wrong, or good and evil, was God-given. Today we call that knowledge "Natural Law." As the Framers began to shape America, Franklin stressed, "There is a natural inclination in mankind to kingly government."[12] All agreed that man, left to his own devices, would look to anarchy and then eventually embrace tyranny if he took the king route. You see, the Framers knew exactly what they were up against because they studied history. "It took the Founding Fathers 180 years (1607 to 1787) to come up with the American formula."[13]

Unlike modern day Washington, D.C., our Founders knew from experience that hearty debate, along with wise give-and-take was necessary if they were ever going to get anything done. They were big picture thinkers, stunningly brilliant, blessed leaders. They were not professional politicians, thank God. They were goal-oriented problem solvers—strategic thinkers. They were men who studied history in depth without modern day tools like Google or Bing. They were well-grounded gentlemen, proven leaders, who knew business, banking and farming first hand. The best our country had to offer answered the call. "When several of the larger states threatened to reject the Constitution, they were invited to ratify the main body of the Constitution but attach suggested amendments. Thus was born America's famous Bill of Rights."[14] How cool is that? I find it fascinating that 189 amendments were suggested and only 10 were ratified. Today, our lot in Washington, D.C. would approve all 189 proposals to ensure that the folks that contributed to their campaigns would remain happy and to ensure that they are voted back into office. The voters call it, "pork" while politicians roll over us by shouting that it is simply "the cost of doing business."

Recently, I heard a Progressive talking head on TV complaining that only gentlemen who had done well for themselves wrote the Constitution. Good grief. Imagine if our dumbest had taken on the task of framing America in to-day's spirit of fairness? Ronald Reagan nailed it when he said: "I have wondered at times about what the Ten Commandments would have looked like if Moses had run them through the U.S. Congress."[15]

Thomas Paine wrote a book by the title *Common Sense*, published in January of 1776. Independence from England was the topic of the day and by April over 120,000 copies were in circulation. Thomas Paine, who published the book anonymously, wrote it to ensure our separation from England. He wrote the book using everyday language and numerous quotes from the Bible. Paine was a catalyst of liberty. His vision was a Republic of Conscience for all humanity. He was a Deist.

> In the end, his prose was common sense. Why should tiny England rule the vastness of a continent? How can colonists expect to gain for-eign support while still professing loyalty to the British king? How much longer can Americans stand for the repeated abuses of the Crown? All these questions led many readers to one answer as the summer of 1776 drew near.[16]

God was viewed as a good and gracious Creator God and the source of all truth. He was part of everyday life and played a large part in the Founders' thought processes. "America's Founders regarded religion as a positive good – something so foundational that they placed it first in the Bill of Rights."[17] On

July the Fourth, 1776 church bells chimed over Philadelphia, proudly proclaiming the Declaration of Independence was now the law of the land. God had His hand on America.

> The American Revolution inaugurated the first government in the world that was based on the principle that sovereignty and rights are in the people and not in the king or the ruling class. It is sometimes said that while European countries located sovereignty in "divine right," America located sovereignty in "the consent of the governed." But this is not correct. Consider Jefferson's famous proclamation, in the Declaration, that "all men are created equal and endowed by their Creator with certain unalienable rights." Notice that Jefferson – who was a man of the Enlightenment, and by no means an orthodox Christian – nevertheless locates the source of equality and rights in a single source: the Creator. Why does he not locate the doctrine of equality in the people, in the consent of the governed? Because never have "all men" or all people ever given their consent to such a proposition. Moreover, even if they did, all people don't become equal – anymore that they become tall or intelligent or morally good-by mutual common agreement!

> What Jefferson means is that all people are equal in having a shared human nature. Being human, they are of equal moral value in the eyes of their Creator. And it is because of this equality that legitimate government derives its authority to rule from the consent of the governed. Far from denying divine right, Jefferson appeals to it. In the American case, however, God sanctions a system in which sovereignty or ultimate authority derives not from a king but from the people. Royal sovereignty under God gives way to common sovereignty under God. America establishes the first government in history that is based on "We the people."[18]

Once again, D'Souza is spot-on. "We hold these truths to be self-evident, that all men are created equal, that they are endowed by their Creator with certain unalienable Rights that among these are Life, Liberty and the pursuit of Happiness."[19] To put it simply, their intent was that all people were to be treated equal by the government. It is a given that people are different in a myriad of ways, but our Founders wished all men to be treated equally under the law. How pure and beautiful is that! They committed to protecting the rights of the weak and the strong, the sick and the healthy, the poor and the wealthy, and most importantly those on the margins of society like widows and orphans. Think about it "America is defined not by blood or birth but by adoption of the nation's Constitution, its laws, and its shared way of life."[20] You can become an American by adoption. Our Founders vision is not shared anywhere else on earth.

"When we use the term *liberty*, for example, we mean the classic definition, famously articulated by Benjamin Franklin: the right to do what is right. Our founders tied freedom – the highest political goal – to moral truth…moral absolutes are our only guarantee to freedom."[21] As mentioned in the Introduction, I had the privilege of being mentored by the late Charles Colson (Breakpoint-The Centurion Program.) Every time we met, Chuck would remind me that without absolute truth we would have chaos. We are living in a culture lacking moral truth. Today's Progressives know that there is often profit in chaos and they use confusion as yet another tool to garnish power and/or favor.

Critical was the concept of States Rights to our Framers. States' Rights was a given to them. The federal judicial system was not to meddle with the states, especially when it came to religious issues. The Founders' intent was for the states to deal with welfare issues, certainly not the federal government. They knew from experience that those nearer the problem (closer to home) most often offer the better and more compassionate solution. I believe schools and homeless shelters, to name a few, are better managed locally than by the Federal Government. Neighbors are far more caring and loving than a bunch of politically motivated bureaucrats whose first priority is to raise enough campaign money to ensure their stay in office. Here is how bureaucrat is defined in the dictionary: "an official who works by a fixed routine without exercising intelligent judgment."[22] You have to love it. I could not have put it better myself. How very sad.

Our Framers also knew what they did NOT want to build into the fabric of our country. Government ownership of major assets was something they wanted to avoid. Prime examples are transportation, natural resources and commerce. The Founders worked to make socialism "unconstitutional." "The American Founders recognized that the moment the government is authorized to start leveling the material possessions of the rich in order to have an "equal distribution of the goods," the government thereafter has the power to deprive ANY of the people of their "equal" rights to enjoy their lives, liberties, and property."[23] Dr. Ravi Zacharias states the obvious: "An inescapable fact is that the Constitution and the Bill of Rights could never have been framed in a Hindu, Muslim, or Buddhist worldview."[24] It is a safe assumption Ravi does not have a "Coexist" sticker on his cars bumper.

The Founders, a group of farmers, viewed our elected representatives as servants of the people they represented. They were to be servants of the people, not self-serving. As mentioned earlier, America with a king sitting on a throne was rejected very early on. They knew from Old Testament history that kings created nothing but trouble and eventual chaos. Our Founders were prophetic as they foresaw population growth as a future problem and decided against a democracy. Bearing in mind a bigger picture, they decided on a republic, thereby utilizing elected representatives. The representatives sent to Washington, D.C. were to be worker bees, like you and me. Normal, everyday citizens were to serve for a while, then return home to allow another his turn at a trip to our nation's Capital. The Founders' vision blurred as today we have "lifers" with no term limits who own second homes in Washington, D.C. Power was to reside with the people, but "we the people" have been cast aside in favor of a powerful, Progressive, power-hungry club with members of both major parties often joining forces to stay in power. Chuck Colson raises an interesting point:

> U.S. Senators were chosen by state legislatures until 1913, when the 17th Amendment made them electable directly by the people, thus turning them into representatives with longer terms and bigger egos. A victory for popular democracy? Maybe! But one wonders if it is a coincidence that the federal government began to expand dramatically at the expense of the states after 1913.[25]

It becomes obvious that the expansion of government is no coincidence given man's love of power, money and self.

The government was to issue money, BUT its purchasing power was to remain fixed. Coins were to be made exclusively of precious metals and paper money was mandated to be backed by gold and silver. Common sense prevailed.

Common good was the overall theme. We will look at government's role and its impact on the money supply in another chapter.

Our Founders were careful to build checks and balances into their experiment. They designed a form of government which breaks down into three equal parts or branches. They deemed three branches necessary due to man's predisposition to sin, which naturally leads to corruption and tyranny. Today, even those who do not believe in the Biblical worldview often agree that the checks and balances built into the system are a net plus. The Framers viewed atheism as a threat as it cuts the heart out of our republic and upon the human rights on which it stands. We are going to see repeatedly in this book that as Progressivism increases, the fallout is a decline in Christianity. We are also going to see repeatedly that as Christianity declines, so will our liberties.

The Constitution is the control mechanism of the government - or should be. States were to be far more powerful than the Federal Government when it came to that which influences the day-to-day lives of the people. The Constitution was clearly designed to limit government's power. Sadly, the federal government's power is increasing exponentially as the Progressives of both parties seek to control more and more. The concepts laid down by our Framers...

> ...have been brazenly ignored in recent decades, with presidents and the federal government usurping authority reserved to the states, ignoring the Constitution when it limits the scope of governmental action, getting into wars without proper congressional authority, politicizing the courts, and so on. These offences have been committed by Democrats and Republicans, progressives and conservatives, although the most flagrant violations are by Democrats and progressives who increasingly don't even pretend to feel inhibited by the Constitution. As a result, we now have a Leviathan state, far from the limited government the Founders envisioned. The government that was set up to protect our rights has in many cases become a danger to our rights.[26]

We all know how checks and balances are supposed to work, but alas today: "Failure to use the checks and balances has also allowed the President to make thousands of new laws, instead of Congress, by issuing executive orders. It has allowed the federal government to impose taxes on the people never contemplated by the Founders or the Constitution."[27]

Normally polite columnist George Will seems to be running out of patience with President Obama as he repeatedly treads destructively on the Constitution.

What philosopher Harvey Mansfield calls "taming the prince" — making executive power compatible with democracy's abhorrence of arbitrary power — has been a perennial problem of modern politics. It is now more urgent in the United States than at any time since the Founders, having rebelled against George III's unfettered exercise of "royal prerogative," stipulated that presidents "shall take care that the laws be faithfully executed."

Serious as are the policy disagreements roiling Washington, none is as important as the structural distortion threatening constitutional equilibrium. Institutional derangement driven by unchecked presidential aggrandizement did not begin with Barack Obama, but his offenses against the separation of powers have been egregious in quantity and qualitatively different.

Regarding immigration, health care, welfare, education, drug policy and more, Obama has suspended, waived and rewritten laws, including the Affordable Care Act. It required the employer mandate to begin this year. But Obama wrote a new law, giving to companies of a certain size a delay until 2016 and stipulating that other employers must certify they will not drop employees to avoid the mandate. Doing so would trigger criminal perjury charges; so he created a new crime, that of adopting a business practice he opposes.

Presidents must exercise *some* discretion in interpreting laws, must have *some* latitude in allocating finite resources to the enforcement of laws and must have *some* freedom to act in the absence of law. Obama, however, has perpetrated more than 40 *suspensions* of laws. Were presidents the sole judges of the limits of their latitude, they would effectively have plenary power to vitiate the separation of powers, the Founders' bulwark against despotism.[28]

Washington, D.C. is gorging away at our liberty. It is gluttonous when it comes to power. How did this cultural chaos happen? I ask myself this question numerous times daily. The late Charles Colson was onto something when he wrote:

Whether a politician cheats on his wife, for example, should have no bearing on his fitness in office, many say. But, a broken vow is a broken vow and reveals a weak character. If a man or a woman cannot be trusted with private moral decisions, how can he or she be trusted with moral decisions affecting the whole society?[29]

If the link between private and public virtue is hard to understand, the problem lies with us, not our Founders. Our culture has forgotten what the Founders knew: The American experiment is a moral, not just a political, exercise. And as such, it assumes certain things to be true about human nature and about the authority of the God of the Bible. Moral values do affect character, and the influence of individual character has an impact on society. Not just with public officials, but in the lives of ordinary citizens. Nowhere is this more evident than in the area of criminal behavior. Though for years conventional wisdom held that racial discrimination, economic deprivation, and environment were the chief causes of crime, leading criminologists and psychologists are now concluding that personal character is the single greatest factor in criminal behavior.[30]

Remember when we took it for granted the Captain would be the last man off a distressed ship? Recently, there have been instances of captains ensuring the survival of #1 to the demise of their passengers. The *Costa Concordia* was grounded on January 13, 2012 - grounded because of sheer folly, showing off, instead of following the discipline of maritime law. The captain of the *Concordia*, Francesco Schettino, was one of the first off, while 32 passengers and one salvage member died along with 64 injured. Far worse, the *MV Sewol* sank April 16, 2014, off South Korea loaded with students. Two hundred and ninety three onboard perished, plus one navy sailor and two civilian divers. The students were told to stay in their cabins while the captain and crew abandoned ship. Character does count. Sometimes it is a matter of life or death.

To add fuel to the fire, how is it possible that a massive piece of legislation, affecting every single citizen and many non-citizens, passed and became law without even being read. Below, please see the link to Nancy Pelosi's eloquent appeal asking Democrats to vote on The Affordable Care Act before reading it. ObamaCare is not the issue at hand. The problem is that we the people no longer run our country when our elected officials rubber-stamp what their party leaders deem to make law. Mention Nancy's quote to anyone, no matter their party affiliation, and more than likely he will shake his head in bewilderment. No one with an ounce of common sense should wish his representative to vote neither for nor against bills he has not read or had his staff mark up and read for him. It is beyond lunacy, it's sheer stupidity. To make matters worse, when our representatives finally read the bill and determine it's not really affordable or workable, they vote to exempt themselves and a few of their closest friends (donors).

(http://www.bing.com/videos/search?q=pelosi+pass+the+bill+to+see+what%27s+in+it&FORM=VIRE2#view=detail&mid=9B8D54F22DC4349CEEA49B8D54F22DC4349CEEA4).

Virtually everyone believed the old health care system required an extensive overhaul. The issue at hand is that of responsibility and accountability. The sheer size of the Affordable Care Act required every word to be read and its repercussions studied in depth (almost 2000 pages). Instead, it was a wham-bam-thank-you-Ma'am-bill that many believe will eventually collapse under its own weight as it crawls through the court system. From the pricing debacle to substandard web site development, the Federal Government has made the case that the closer to home the governing, the better for the governed. Each state should set up its own system designed and administered by neighbors. Imagine, nearly every person's healthcare was determined by a straight party line vote without being read. All who voted for the bill should be fired on principle and their pensions donated to the indigent sick.

Further, how stupid can we get when we turn and then re-elect the puppets who vote the party line without understanding what they are voting on. Politics over people, mass corruption and self-empowerment has created massive gridlock in Washington, D.C. Trickle down politics (Keystone Pipeline, fracking) have slowed down innovation and the economy. Its far reaching destruction has yet to run its course. Our Founders had common sense and knew that to borrow money was borrowing against the future. Especially ill-advised is borrowing from enemies of the U.S.A.

Nancy Pelosi's Pied Piper video got me thinking about political parties. In many ways, they have robbed the average American of his or her power to think for themselves. Granted, the following statements could be viewed as glittering generalities but it seems to me obvious that:

- most union types vote Democratic,
- most small business owners vote Republican,
- most climate change types vote Democratic,
- most states rights types vote Republican,
- most Afro Americans vote Democratic,
- most Protestants vote Republican,
- most Catholics vote Democratic,
- most Evangelicals vote Republican or opt to stay home as in the election of 2012.

Sometimes it seems like our elections are more about voting blocs made up of nationalities, religions, race, sex, jobs etc. than issues. It all boils down to a "We" versus "They" mentality. Lately, I have come to realize no one wins except an ever-expanding, powerful, forceful centralized government, run by career politicians, greedily printing more money. The printing press to Washington, D.C. is the empty gift box that just keeps on giving. They are going to print us into default if "we the people" don't demand they stop the presses soon. I believe we should vote only for those who are in favor of a balanced budget amendment. If you are vocal and pressure Washington, D.C. to balance the budget, the current lot laughs in your face. They know what they are doing is wrong, yet they succumb to the pull of power and favor because it feels so good being them. They are the epitome of the "it's all about me" Progressive worldview.

Our Founders did not wish for nor write into the experiment the concept of parties. "A sure sign of the great novelty of political parties was that the Constitution had established that the runner-up in the presidential election would become the vice president."[31] "The vice presidency was given little consideration by the Framers of the Constitution. Some of them were opposed to having the position at all, so as to compromise it was made into a weak office, made possible by a last-minute insertion into the Constitution and given just one explicit duty – to preside over the Senate."[32] Our Framers knew that the purpose of the government was to protect our God-given rights. Since these rights and liberties come from our Creator, it follows that it would have been inconceivable to our Founders to reject God and ban Him from public life. How far we have strayed and continue to do so. George Washington started the tradition of a Presidential oath of office. Washington added to the end of the oath, "So help me God."

Our parents taught us patriotism in a myriad of ways. My mother worked hard to instill in my brother Mark, and me love of country. She loved flags, parades and all sorts of patriotic costume jewelry. We loved and respected our parents because we knew we would be punished if we broke a rule. Our parents would be called "mean-spirited" today because they set limits. They ruled the roost. They had the final advice on everything. Yes, everything! There were no low-slung trousers or shorts, flip-flop wearing, tattoos, or halters showing midriffs as we headed off to school. There was no printed dress code sent to parents by the school nor need of one as all of our moms seemed to have the same parenting rulebook naturally embedded in their brain. Our mom inspected us as we marched out the door. Once again, common sense prevailed.

Our parents worked hard to make things special and meaningful. Thanksgiving, back in the day, was more about thanks than turkey and football. Come autumn, we would learn about the pilgrims at school and at church. We were taught to be grateful for the sacrifices the pilgrims made and thankful for the sacrifices that many other great Americans made especially those who served in the armed forces. One Thanksgiving, I flew home from college planning to watch TV, eat great food (I was on the institutional meal plan at college), drive my parents' car and catch up on sleep. Much to my chagrin, I was informed that my mom had invited three or four soldiers over from a nearby Naval base for Thanksgiving Day. She could not stand that they were away from loved ones on a holiday, without home cooking and appreciative company. I looked at it as a terrible inconvenience, an invasion of my privacy, and worst of all they were nearly bald. What a jerk I was! These young brave men were soon to be deployed to Vietnam, probably scared out of their minds, and I felt inconvenienced by them enjoying a home cooked meal. That was not one of my prouder moments.

All of my life my parents picked up the bill at restaurants should a member of the armed forces be dining within eye shot. Of course, payment was anonymous but with a note, delivered by the server, thanking them for their service. Today's ruling Progressive Secularists might require mom to obtain some sort of food serving permit before she opened her home to strangers. No doubt, they would prefer the soldiers go without than put them "at risk" from a patriotic mom's home cooking. Later in our book we will flesh out these comments.

I believe that for national identity to be salient in the midst of our changing society, we need to promote a recommitment to our creeds, a respect for human history, and a proper role for patriotism, rooted in love of neighbor…our national creed, the Declaration of Independence.[33]

Charles Colson

Chuck Colson was spot-on when he wrote of our national identity. The Progressives would like nothing more than to erase the Red, White and Blue in favor of United Nations blue. If you think I am exaggerating, then read on:

Holder: International Law Trumps The Constitution!

Every now and then, news breaks in the Obama administration that is so stereotypical, it is actually depressing. You might want to sit down for this.

Attorney General Eric Holder, made infamous by Operation Fast and Furious, is currently arguing before the Supreme Court that United Nations treaties trump the United States Constitution.

That's right. The sitting Attorney General, charged with upholding and defending the Constitution, is arguing before the highest court that international law is in fact the law of the land.

The case in question, Bond v. United States, is actually pretty ridiculous. The defendant is charged with using a toxic substance to harass a friend who was having an affair with her husband. Under the law, this case would normally be handled at the State-level. But Federal prosecutors instead charged Bond with violating the Chemical Weapons Convention. This would be like taking a perpetrator of a domestic hate crime and instead charging him or her with genocide.

This case is basically a complex liberal experiment to see how far they can push the boundaries regarding the enforcement of international law. An Obama administration victory in this case could have huge ramifications for other contentious issues like abortion, citizenship, and even the Second Amendment…

… Bond v. United States represents a grave risk to the sovereignty of this great country and the supremacy of the U.S. Constitution. Everyone always posits that the liberals want to replace the Constitution with U.N. law, but no one actually expected them to try to.

If the Courts rule that international law is law of the land, and if the Executive branch is more than willing to implement this ruling, then only the Congress can stand against this rising tyranny.

A lot of times, Congress' power can be overstated. But the Constitution's system of checks and balances exist for a reason. If one or two branches of government fall to tyranny, then a third branch would still remain to herald the cause of liberty. With the way the Supreme Court has been ruling lately, and Obama's burning desire to shred the Constitution, the Congress is all that stands between state sovereignty and global governance.

Unfortunately more often than not, Congressmen and Senators wouldn't recognize creeping tyranny if it slapped them in the face.

That's where we come in. Believe it or not, we have reached a point in our history where we actually have to plead with our representatives to defend the Constitution from its domestic and foreign enemies…

…Most of the time, slippery slope arguments are overblown. But there's no exaggeration to this. Even when the Senate refused to ratify the U.N. Arms Treaty, Obama had Secretary of State John Kerry sign it anyway. Talk about defiance![34]

In the 60's my mom's car sported a bumper sticker "Get us out of the United Nations." I never thought much about it. Mom's sticker goes to show you how long the United Nations has posed a threat to our sovereignty.

2

THE PROGRESSIVE GAME PLAN

As discussed, a Progressive is a Liberal sporting a new nametag.

Bing Dictionary defines Liberal a couple of ways:

"1. broad-minded: tolerant of different views and standards of behavior in others

2. progressive politically or socially: favoring gradual reform, especially political reforms that extend democracy, distribute wealth more evenly, and protect the personal freedom of the individual"

Progressives consider themselves "radicals" and attempt to take credit for all that is good in America. Today's two shining stars of the Progressive movement are President Barack Obama and former Secretary of State and Senator Hillary Clinton. Both are followers of the late Saul Alinsky. Their radical Progressive guru describes their movement:

> America's radicals are to be found wherever and whenever America moves close to the fulfillment of its democratic dream. Whenever America's hearts are breaking, there American radicals were and are. America was built by its radicals. The hope and future of America lies with its radicals.[35]

A humble lot, aren't they?

"By the time Hillary entered Wellesley College in 1965, she was a committed leftist…She had met Saul Alinsky in high school, but she renewed her association with him in college, inviting him to speak at Wellesley, and writing her undergraduate thesis on him."[36] Hillary's senior thesis at Wellesley College (class of 1969) examined the community organizing tactics of Saul Alinsky.

But rarely has it been read, because for the eight years of Bill Clinton's presidency it was locked away. As forbidden fruit, the writings of a 21-year-old college senior, examining the tactics of radical community organizer Saul D. Alinsky, have gained mythic status among her critics…[37]

Hillary's thesis is not in public circulation. The stifling of one's thesis is unique for a First Lady, Senator, Presidential candidate or Secretary of State. Rank clearly has its Progressive privileges. Transparency seems to be a non-issue to Hillary. She considered working with one of the Alinsky's organizations but decided instead to attend Yale Law School.

Barbara Olson, the conservative lawyer and commentator, used an Alinsky quote to open every chapter of her 1999 book, "Hell to Pay: The Unfolding Story of Hillary Rodham Clinton." Olson, who died in the Sept. 11 terror attacks, had charged in her book that the thesis was locked away because Clinton "does not want the American people to know the extent to which she internalized and assimilated the beliefs and methods of Saul Alinsky…"

…Rodham closed her thesis by emphasizing that she reserved a place for Alinsky in the pantheon of social action — seated next to Martin Luther King, the poet-humanist Walt Whitman, and Eugene Debs, the labor leader now best remembered as the five-time Socialist Party candidate for president.[38]

A decade later, another political science major started out on the path that Hillary Rodham had rejected, going to work for a group in the Alinsky mold. That was Barack Obama, who was elected to be a U.S. senator from Illinois and her leading opponent for the Democratic nomination for President in 2008. After attending Columbia University, he worked as an organizer on the South Side of Chicago for the Developing Communities Project. Obama and others of the post-Alinsky generation described their work in the 1990 book "After Alinsky: Community Organizing in Illinois," in which Obama wrote that he longed for ways to close the gap between community organizing and national politics. After three years of organizing, he turned to Harvard Law School and then the Illinois legislature.[39]

"Obama learned from Alinsky how to convert radical ideology into political power; in other words, how to win and retain high office."[40] Obama also rubbed fundraising and ideology elbows with Bill Ayers. It seems our President considers it no big deal to wine and dine with the infamous 1970's Pentagon bomber who on national TV (The Kelly File on Fox News Network) recently claimed he, under the right circumstances, might revert to violence again. "Today Ayers is a respected professor of education at the University of Illinois at Chicago. Normally terrorists get sent to prison or Guantanamo; in this case, he got tenure."[41] Ayers proudly proclaims that the education system is the best form of activism. Win the hearts and minds of today's youth and you will get all the hope and change needed to create a borderless utopian world. Bill Ayers' wife, who also has tenure at a top US university, famously told followers to "kill your parents."[42]

Progressive activists such as Obama/Clinton types are doing a great deal of harm to our once great country. Many agree with me that the United States is no longer viewed as one of the world's policy makers. Instead, the world is looking to the United Nations or Angela Merkel, the Chancellor of Germany, for guidance. America is looked to for one thing and one thing only – cold hard cash. We have become the world's ATM. The world's cash cow. Foreign leaders know we are no longer willing to draw a meaningful line in the sand. We have ceded precious sovereignty to the United Nations and will continue to cede more if the Progressives continue to rule. Neither our word nor our treaties are viewed as rock solid. This is all part of the plan. Progressives' wish is for America to become smaller and the world to become larger. As I write this book there are numerous illegal aliens flooding our borders. The Federal Government is busing them to states and dropping them off, in some instances without alerting the local authorities. Big government is the engine behind the Progressive power grab as they seek ways to amass control.

The tactics Progressives utilize are as stunning as they are diabolical. Is my use of the term diabolical too strong a word or too "mean spirited?" The Bing dictionary defines diabolical as "of devil: connected with the devil or devil worship." Unbelievably, Alinsky dedicated his book to the devil.

One can see Lucifer's influence in Alinsky's contention that "ethical standards must be elastic to stretch with the times." Alinsky wrote that morality and ethics were fine for those who don't seek to improve the world for the better; But for those who do, the ends always justifies the means.[43] (Emphasis mine)

Saul Alinsky wrote two books from which I am going to quote from to close out this chapter: *Rules for Radicals; A Pragmatic Primer for Realistic Radicals*[44] and *Reveille for Radicals.*[45] I pray the quotes below will open your eyes as they did mine. These quotes exemplify the way they play politics.

The Judeo-Christian rules of our Founders are very different from the rules for radicals. Roger will have a lot to say about this later in our book.

From *Rules for Radicals*...

- "The organizer's job is to inseminate an invitation for himself, to agitate, introduce ideas, get people pregnant with hope and a desire for change and to identify you as the person most qualified for this purpose." Pg. 103

  Barack Obama and his team took this rule and turned it into his campaign slogan – "Hope and Change."

- "The middle classes are numb, bewildered, scared into silence. They don't know what, if anything they can do. This is the job for today's radical-to fan the embers of hopelessness onto a flame to fight." Pg. 194

  The Progressives have succeeded in silencing many in the middle class who are "numb, bewildered, and scared..." Fight for what? More "Hope and Change?"

- "...our concern is with the tactic of taking; how the Have-Nots can take power from the Haves." Pg. 126

- "Ethical standards must be elastic to stretch with the times." Pg. 30/31
  Lying is one of the ethics the Progressives employ to carry the day. The best current example is the IRS debacle. Lois Lerner hides behind the Fifth Amendment then turns around and seemly lies about her computer and phone records.
- "To me *ethics* is doing what is right for the most." Pg. 33
  Right is right and wrong is wrong – I give you abortion.
- "...rule of ethics of means and ends is that you do what you can with what you have and clothe it with moral garments." Pg. 36
  Women's right to choose sounds so ethical and moral until you counter with the A-word. Abortion.
- "The organizer is in a true sense reaching for the highest level for which man can reach-to create, to be a "great creator," to play God." Pg. 61
- "The function of an organizer is to raise questions that agitate, that break through the accepted pattern." Pg. 72
- Organizer – "...nothing is sacred...He is challenging, insulting, agitation, discrediting. He stirs unrest." Pg. 73
  Our President has shown the American people in many ways that "nothing is sacred."
- Manipulation is the name of the game. "...just as a teacher manipulates..." Pg. 92
  Alinsky's game plan zeroes in on the classroom. They seek to indoctrinate their worldview using our schools.
- "In a fight almost anything goes. It almost reaches the point where you stop to apologize if a chance blow lands *above* the belt." Pg. 130
  Incredible when one considers hitting below the belt the normal way to do business.

From *Reveille for Radicals*

- It is a tactic "...to burn one's bridges because you're never going back anyway..." Pg. viii
  Little wonder our foreign policy is in such shambles.
- "...morality is largely a rationalization of the point you happen to occupy in the power pattern at a given time." Pg. x
  In other words, "morality" is whatever works.

- "America's radicals are to be found wherever and whenever America moves close to the fulfillment of its democratic dream. Whenever America's hearts are breaking, there American radicals were and are. America was built by its radicals. The hope and future of America lies with its radicals." Pg. 15

  Do you think our Founders would agree with Alinsky?

- "Society has good reason to fear the radical. Every shaking advance of mankind toward equality and justice has come from the radical. He hits, he hurts, he is dangerous." Pg. 21

  Talk about inflated egos.

- "Throughout Western civilization, radicals tied their destiny to the organized labor movement...The labor movement has been as much of an ideological foundation to all left-wing thinkers as the Ten Commandments and the Golden Rule are to devout religionists." Pg. 24

  Isn't this a provocative statement? Left-wing thinkers are ideologically linked to the labor movement as the Christians are to the Ten Commandments and the Golden Rule.

- "We have said that we must surely end war or it will surely end us. It is obvious that if the people of the world are free, informed, participating to the fullest degree, working together co-operatively, possessed of an understanding of the problems and those of their fellow men, completely aware of that simple truth that the welfare of one is contingent on the welfare of all *others, secure in a faith in themselves and in their fellow men, committed to ideals of human* decency, then there would be no wars." Pg. 41

  Coexist is the bumper sticker encompassing the paragraph above. Socialism sounds good but it never has worked and never will. People want to be free.

- "The radical cannot suffer *personal* defeat because in a sense he is selfless." Pg. 90

  Stunning how "selfless" Barack Obama is, isn't it!

- "The democratic way of life is predicated upon faith in the masses of mankind, yet few of the leaders of democracy really possess faith in the people." Pg. 192

The "Nanny State" continues to grow because we need big government to tend to us. The lot in Washington D.C. really believe they are the smartest people on earth and are in power to "rule."

- "…today much of organized religion is materialistically solvent but spiritually bankrupt." Pg. 200

  Alinsky may have a point here which I am confident Roger will address later on in our book.

- "We find ourselves in a world where people are dying of malnutrition while here most of us are dieting." Pg. 205

- "…the general lack of leadership in America-is ominous for the democratic future." Pg. 211

- "The welfare establishment has mushroomed to the extent that it must now be classified as one of urban America's major industries. So many thousands of people and millions of dollars may be an incalculable asset, but may also pose a singular problem, if the industry pursues a course that is self-protective and either irrelevant or in contradiction to the wishes and demands of the people." Pg. 216

  Yes, welfare is "one of urban America's major industries" and growing by the minute. The influx of illegals is compounding the issue.

- The peoples of the world must live together, and the world is shrinking by the hour. Living together means that the multiple ethical systems and values around the earth must be synthesized into certain universals acceptable to the people of the world." Pg. 222

  One world, one big border called Earth, one currency, one flag, one god as we synthesize into "certain universals." America is big-hearted, but it cannot sustain the world.

Reading Alinsky's books have opened my eyes as to how and why President Obama conducts business as he does. The infamous "What difference does it make?" Benghazi comment made by Hillary now makes sense. Sadly, a few dead Americans seem merely a means to her agenda's end, a bump in the road to Utopia.

Claiming to be transparent while handcuffing numerous inquiries, like the IRS scandal, is another means to an end. The White House no longer tries to deal with many issues; it simply turns its back to them and ignores inquiries they deem unworthy of a reply. The arrogance is stunning! Before writing this book, I could not for the life of me understand, why the Press echoes the Presidential agenda even when the narrative is obviously false. Now I understand. It's all about POWER! The elite media is assisting with the construction of Utopia. This fact contributes to the lack of investigative journalism and the subjugation of the citizenry.

3

PROGRESSIVE ATTACKS

Political Correctness

Robert George, in a recent article dealing with academic freedom states:

> The interrogative attitude will flourish only under conditions of freedom. It can be smothered by speech codes and the like, to be sure, but also in less obvious ways. It can be smothered when well-qualified scholars, teachers, and academic administrators are denied positions in institutions that claim to be nonpartisan and nonsectarian, or when they are denied tenure or promotion or are subjected to discriminatory treatment. It can be smothered by an atmosphere of political correctness.[46]

Let's take a step back and define "political correctness" before we tackle how it is used as a tool against our right to freedom of speech.

- **Political correctness** (adjectivally, **politically correct**; both forms commonly abbreviated to **PC**) is a contentious term that today commonly refers to enforced language, ideas, or policies that address perceived discrimination against political, social or economical groups ("protected classes").[47]

- conforming to a belief that language and practices which could offend political sensibilities (as in matters of sex or race) should be eliminated[48]
- **political correctness** – avoidance of expressions or actions that can be perceived to exclude or marginalize or insult people who are socially disadvantaged or discriminated against.[49]

An excellent example of political correctness run amok is governmental overreach by the U.S. Patent and Trademark Office concerning the "Redskins." George Will lays out the Redskin issue superbly.

Amanda Blackhorse, a Navajo who successfully moved a federal agency to withdraw trademark protections from the Washington Redskins because it considers the team's name derogatory, lives on a reservation where Navajos root for the Red Mesa High School Redskins. She opposes this name; the Native Americans who picked and retain it evidently do not.

The U.S. Patent and Trademark Office acted on a 1946 law banning trademarks that "may disparage" persons. "May" gives the agency latitude to disregard evidence regarding how many people actually feel disparaged or feel that others should feel disparaged. Blackhorse speaks of "the majority of Native American people who have spoken out on this." This would seem implausible even if a 2004 poll had not found that 90 percent of Native Americans were not offended by the Redskins' name. A 2013 AP-GfK poll showed that 79 percent of Americans of all ethnicities opposed changing it, and just 18 percent of "nonwhite football fans" favored changing it.

The federal agency acted in the absence of general or Native American revulsion about "Redskins," and probably because of this absence. Are the Americans who are paying attention to this controversy comfortable with government saying, in effect, that if people are not offended, they should be, so government must decide what uses of language should be punished?

The name "Redskins" is more problematic than, say, that of the Chicago Blackhawks or Cleveland Indians presumably because "Redskins" refers to skin pigmentation. People offended by this might be similarly distressed if they knew that "Oklahoma" is a compound of two Choctaw words meaning "red" and "people." Blackhorse, however, has two larger objections.

She says "someone" once told her that teams' mascots "are meant to be ridiculed," "to be toyed with," "to be pushed around and disrespected" and "have stuff thrown at them." She should supplement the opinion of that someone with information from persons more knowledgeable. But she considers "any team name that references Native Americans" an injurious "appropriation of our culture." Has an "appropriation" been committed by the University of Utah and Florida State University even though they have the approval of the respective tribes for their teams' nicknames, the Utes and Seminoles?[50]

Somehow, I think our Founders never contemplated the Federal Government using a powerful agency like its U.S. Patent and Trademark Office to advance an ideology.

The Bing dictionary defines ideology as…

- system of social beliefs: a closely organized system of beliefs, values, and ideas forming the basis of a social, economic, or political philosophy or program
- meaningful belief system: a set of beliefs, values, and opinions that shapes the way a person or a group such as a social class thinks, acts, and understands the world[51]

Attack on Freedom of Speech on College Campuses

Recently, former Secretary of State Condoleezza Rice was all but physically forced to withdraw from giving the commencement speech at Rutgers University because of her work in the Bush Administration. Can't you hear the outcry from so-called enlightened students and professors? Loud mouth professors who probably have never worked anywhere but in a sterile campus environment sur-rounded by adoring students. Tenured professors live in a protected world with no fear of being laid off or fired. They are set for life. College is like a second womb in which professors, insulated by tenure, provide progressive nourish-ment to our future leaders. Don't think that Condoleezza Rice stands alone as Smith and Brandeis also had a change in the batting order of commencement speakers in 2014. Isn't it stunning that an African-American woman, whose alma maters are the University of Denver and Notre Dame, who served as Provost of Stanford University, United States National Security Advisor and United States Secretary of State, would find herself a pariah at Rutgers because, in my opinion, she has the audacity to NOT be a Liberal Democrat. How dare she! Ms. Rice does not fit the liberal mold precisely and nothing else matters...absolutely noth-ing. The PC (Politically Correct) leftist secular way is the only way or one quickly finds oneself persona non grata on the speaking circuit. If you want your child to be a leftist thinking soldier fighting for the political correctness cause then, blow the lock off your wallet and send him or her to Rutgers. The leadership at Rutgers should be ashamed of their unfounded and biased treatment of Ms. Rice.[52]

I had to laugh when the second invitee commencement speaker at Haverford College, William G. Bowen, a former president of Princeton, turned the table on the graduating class. It seems the first speaker, Robert J. Birgeneau, a former chancellor of the University of California Berkeley, found himself dethroned from the speaking engagement because in 2011 he had the audacity to call in the UC Berkley police to handle students protesting the cost of attending. Mr. Bowden turned the table on the radicals:

> A group of more than 40 students and three Haverford professors -
> all Berkeley alums - objected to Birgeneau's appearance and receipt of an
> honorary degree, noting that many of them had participated in Occupy
> protests as well and wanted to stand in solidarity with Berkeley students.
> They wrote a letter to Birgeneau, urging him to meet nine conditions,
> including publicly apologizing, supporting reparations for the victims,
> and writing a letter to Haverford students explaining his position on the
> events and "what you learned from them."[53]

What a bunch of arrogant twits. Forty activist students and three ex-Berkley alums carried the day at Haverford.

Bowden gave the graduating class a lesson on freedom of speech when he said,

> In my view, they should have encouraged him to come and engage in a genuine discussion, not to come, tail between his legs, to respond to an indictment that a self-chosen jury had reached without hearing counter-arguments.[54]

Bowden stated he felt the change in speakers was not a win but a defeat for the Quaker college and all it stands for. Not surprisingly, when the pressure was off and students were free to think for themselves, the audience of around 2,800 gave him a standing ovation.[55]

Good for Bowen and plaudits to the 2,800 who saw through the Liberals' Political Correct agenda.

In an article cited earlier, Professor George reminds us that the president of Harvard "can be brought down for a thought crime..."[56] Remember Larry Summers fell for asking an intellectual question whether differences between men and women, when it comes to scientific achievement, might have something to do with not only nature but nurture. How dare he raise a politically incorrect issue? Fire his butt screeched leftist students and the mainstream media. I wonder how many tenured professors at Harvard are pro-life or pro-traditional marriage. Better yet, I wonder how many tenured professors at Harvard would admit to being pro-life or pro-traditional marriage. It is a one-way street until we destroy political correctness through the ballot box. We must take a stand for Truth. Freedom of speech is non-existent on many college campuses. The more elite the institution – the more this is true.

> Should academic freedom be boundless? Of course not. And the legitimate scope of expression is obviously narrower in institutions that are founded on particular religious and moral principles than it is in institutions that proclaim themselves to be nonsectarian and nonpartisan. But the scope of freedom, as a value that is ordered to truth, must be generous—especially in the academy, where free inquiry,

exploration, and experimentation are often essential to insight and richer understanding.[57]

Today, the orthodoxy of PC holds tenure while The Truth is silenced.

Attack on Excellence

While Progressives fight to level the playing field, parents fight for excellence and the American dream.

"A Rhode Island school district that had come under criticism for canceling a night for honors students over concerns that the event would be too "exclusive" is <u>reversing</u> its stance."[58] The numerous initial reports all read similar to:

> A Rhode Island middle school is canceling its long-running "Honors Night" event for exceptional students, because school officials are afraid its "exclusive nature" will make others feel left out...

> Some parents are afraid the change will discourage kids from working harder to try and make the honor list, the station reported. "How else are they supposed to learn coping skills, not just based on success, but relative failure?" asked parent Joe Kosloski.[59]

In the case of Archie R. Cole Middle School, the school administrators eventually acquiesced to the parents' outcry. A local ABC affiliate reported the schools' defense. Principal Alexis Meyer and Assistant Principal Dan Seger stated, "...members of the school community have long expressed concerns related to the exclusive nature of Honors Night,"[60] Give me a break. Their concerns are to make sure no one's feelings are hurt. It's all about feeling good about ourselves and not about academic excellence. Once again, and a thread throughout our book, parents know more and care more about their children than school administrators.

Attack on Truth

"Liar, liar pants on fire" is a phrase that children scream whenever one thinks that the other is lying. Hot pants revisionists are working hard to undermine America's history to justify their secular pursuits. "Recent Supreme Court cases seem to reflect a determination to strip even the thin veneer of religious signs and symbols from culture."[61] Journalist Michael Snyder sums it up quite nicely:

> When I was a little boy, my public school teachers were still teaching the founding fathers that were involved in the Boston Tea Party were great patriots that were trying to throw off the vile oppression of the British.
>
> But now many public schools are openly referring to them as "terrorists". For example, down in Texas a public school curriculum known as CSCOPE is being widely used. The following is from a CSCOPE lesson plan labeled "World History Unit 12 Lesson 07"...
>
>> A local militia, believed to be a terrorist organization, attacked the property of private citizens today at our nation's busiest port. Although no one was injured in the attack, a large quantity of merchandise, considered to be valuable to its owners and loathsome to the perpetrators, was destroyed. The terrorists, dressed in disguise and apparently intoxicated, were able to escape into the night with the help of local citizens who harbor these fugitives and conceal their identities from the authorities. It is believed that the terrorist attack was a response to the policies enacted by the occupying country's government. Even stronger policies are anticipated by the local citizens.
>
> Of course thanks to a great outcry this particular lesson plan is now considered "outdated" and is not supposed to be used any longer, but this is just one example of the kind of things that are being taught.[62]

Once again, the parents charged forward and pulled the plug on the leftist attack on Truth.

We all know the Boston Tea Party (1773) was, in historical fact, a raid on three ships by a group of Massachusetts colonists dressed as Indians. They tossed three boatloads of tea into Boston Harbor. The colonists felt they were being taxed without representation and staged a revolt against England's tyranny. I was taught as a child and still believe that the Boston Tea Party was a major step leading to the American Revolution. Have any facts changed? No, educators' worldview is what has changed. Now teachers frame American patriots as terrorists. The issue at hand is perspective (worldview). Or to put it another way, the issue is Truth. I strive to view everything through Judeo-Christian lenses while secularist educators' point of view funnels through one world religion lenses. A-one-god-fits all point of view:

> ... those that are seeking to promote a "one world religion" want our children to believe that all religions are "different paths to God" and that we need to bring all of the religions of the world together for the sake of "global harmony".[63]

Much is made of the fact that Ben Franklin called some of the founders "Deists." Deism is a school of thought whereby God created the world and all that is in it and now watches it from afar. Deists believe God built into the fabric of creation and man certain natural and moral laws. Certainly, men who believed God created men and women with a predisposition toward moral laws are not atheists as militant secularists would have us believe. The bottom line is that the vast majority of our Framers were men who considered themselves devout Christians.

> In May of 1854, the Congress of the United States passed a resolution in the House which declared: 'A great vital and conservative element in our system is the belief of our people in the pure doctrines in divine truths in the gospel of Jesus Christ.' On July 13, 1787, the Continental Congress enacted the Northwest Ordinance which stated: 'Religion, morality, and knowledge, being necessary to good government and the happiness of mankind, schools and the means of education shall be forever encouraged.' On August 7, 1789, after the final agreement on the final wording of the Bill of Rights, the newly formed Congress re-enacted the Northwest Ordinance. On September 25, 1789, Congress unanimously approved a resolution asking President George Washington to proclaim a National Day of Thanksgiving, and then on October 3, 1789 George Washington proclaimed a National Day of Thanksgiving. Congress approved a Joint Resolution which added "under God" to the *Pledge of Allegiance*. On July 20, 1956, Congress passed a joint Resolution, which adopted Rep. Charles E. Bennett's bill providing the official motto, "In God We Trust.[64]

Crafting our national holidays was hardly the work of atheists or agnostics as today's revisionists would have our youth believe.

Interestingly enough, the term "wall of separation between church and state" is NOT in the Constitution. Thomas Jefferson never said it nor believed it. As a matter of fact, to be ignored by revisionists, "On three occasions, President Jefferson signed into law federal land grants specifically to promote proselytizing among native American Indians."[65] There are numerous other examples, but hopefully I have made my point.

I listen far too much to talking heads on TV. Thankfully, I missed Eleanor Clift's stunning and provocative comments about U.S. Ambassador Stevens's death in Benghazi.

> I would like to point out that Ambassador Stevens was not 'murdered,'" Clift exclaimed (even adding air quotes for good measure), "he died of smoke inhalation in a safe room in that CIA installation."

> Fellow panelists quickly took issue with her statements, including Pat Buchanan, who fired back: "It was a terrorist attack, Eleanor. He was murdered in a terrorist attack."

> Clift dug in her heels, further insisting that Benghazi was an "opportunistic terrorist attack" with an anti-Muslim video as its catalyst. In addition, she noted earlier that the Benghazi issue "animates the right-wing of the Republican party."

> "It's still a CIA [outpost]," Clift added. "And if you're going to put people on trial, we should put David Petraeus on trial, not Hillary Clinton."[66]

This is a spot-on example of Progressives saying anything to get to where they want to go. In this case, our Ellie considered covering Hillary's missteps and abrogation of her duty well worth revising history and stomping on Truth. Her disrespect and disregard for our Ambassador, his brave guards and our military is infuriating.

It is hard for me to categorize the data I am using as examples because many of the Progressive attacks overlap. The recent Veterans Administration cover up is an example of overreach, abuse and revisionism by the Progressives in power. The attack on truth seems to be a non-issue to the Obama Administration.

About two years ago, Brian Turner took a job as a scheduling clerk at a Veterans Affairs health clinic in Austin. A few weeks later, he said, a supervisor came by to instruct him how to cook the books.

"The first time I heard it was actually at my desk. They said, 'You gotta zero out the date. The wait time has to be zeroed out,'" Turner recalled in a phone interview. He said "zeroing out" was a trick to fool the VA's own accountability system, which the bosses up in Washington used to monitor how long patients waited to see the doctor.

This is how it worked: A patient asked for an appointment on a specific day. Turner found the next available time slot. But, often, it was many days later than the patient had wanted.

Would that later date work? If the patient said yes, Turner canceled the whole process and started over. This time, he typed in that the patient had wanted that later date all along. So now, the official wait time was... a perfect zero days.

It was a lie, of course. But it seemed to be a very important lie, one that the system depended on. "Two to three times a month, you would hear something about it," Turner said — another reminder from supervisors to "zero out." "It wasn't a secret at all."

But all this was apparently a secret to Secretary Eric K. Shinseki, perched 12 levels above Turner in the VA's towering bureaucracy. Somewhere underneath Shinseki — among the undersecretaries and deputy undersecretaries and bosses and sub-bosses — the fact that clerks were cheating the system was lost.[67]

Secretary Shinseki resigned shortly after. It seems it never crossed his mind that subordinates would lie to him. Washington, D.C. today is a culture of cover-ups and chaos. The most stunning to me is probably the IRS cover up and Lois Lerner.

Attack on the Red, White and Blue

When I was young, we all revered the astronauts who landed on the moon. They were the "American Idols" of my day. Not too long ago, our country was exuberantly patriotic and proud of it. President John F. Kennedy cast a vision to the scientific community which became reality on July 16, 1969, when Apollo 11 blasted off. Four days later, the country, bursting with patriotism, celebrated Armstrong's and Aldrin's epic landing on the moon. America was the world's innovator and proud of it. The Apollo Crew were American space explorers who risked their lives for their country. They were pioneers cast from the mold of the Puritans that founded our great Republic. The USA was the leader not only in passenger aviation, expanding routes around the world, but now, space travel was a reality. How proud we were of NASA and our astronauts. Fast forward and programs like space travel have been abandoned in favor entitlements.

The landing of the astronauts on the moon is etched into my mind like the collapsing World Trade Center Towers of 9/11. I can see both images in my mind's eye as though it were yesterday. My, have things changed. Obama is not at all like Kennedy with his eyes on American exceptionalism. Instead, President Obama has dismantled our space program in favor of a one world utopia.

> Now that the space shuttle program has been retired, NASA can start focusing on its primary mission: reaching out to the Muslim world...

> It is quite sad to see how NASA has suffered in the last four decades. Instead of excitement about the space program, there is a sense that it is coming to an end with the retirement of the space shuttle.

> Who could have predicted that NASA would no longer explore space, the final frontier? Despite all of the technology breakthroughs in the last four decades, our country is currently incapable of replicating what was done in 1969, sending an astronaut to the Moon.

> NASA is a perfect example of a government bureaucracy that became inefficient and top-heavy with management, and lost sight of its most important objectives. Back in the 1960s, with the advent of the Apollo program, NASA was an adept and nimble agency, able to meet Kennedy's ambitious challenge.

> Today, we have a President who is not asking the agency to shoot for the stars. Instead, Barack Obama has other goals for NASA, such as studying the so-called problem of manmade global warming.

Liberals like President Obama do not want astronauts reaching for the stars, they want rocket scientists to place their focus on Planet Earth, studying global temperatures and producing research that will support green energy initiatives.

Incredibly, President Obama's other primary mission for NASA is to reach out to the Muslim world. Last year, NASA Administrator Charles Bolden told Al Jazeera television that President Obama gave him three primary tasks: encourage children to learn about math and science, improve relations with foreign nations and "perhaps foremost, he wanted me to find a way to reach out to the Muslim world and engage much more with dominantly Muslim nations to help them feel good about their historic contribution to science … and math and engineering."

It is ludicrous for NASA to be focused on Muslim outreach or boosting the self-esteem of the Islamic world. NASA should not be an arm of the State Department. It is just another indication of how far the agency has strayed from its primary mission.

For the foreseeable future, our country will have to hitchhike on the Russian Soyuz capsule to reach the International Space Station at a cost of $60 million per passenger. The concrete Bush administration plans to reach the Moon and Mars have been scrapped and future space initiatives seem very questionable. While Bolden boasts of a future mission to land an astronaut on an asteroid, there is no space vehicle in production to carry out these unfocused goals. In the meantime, the Hubble telescope will never be serviced again and, according to former NASA administrator Michael Griffin, our country's space flight programs are at "an end for the indefinite future."

Several companies in the private sector are working on plans to send tourists into low Earth orbit, but none of these companies can replicate the achievements of the space shuttle program. NASA cannot be replaced by entrepreneurial ventures with no track record.

Space exploration is a worthy goal for our country to pursue. In the past 50 years, we have achieved amazing technological advances and been able to inspire decades of young schoolchildren with the NASA program.

Today, the program is literally Earth-bound and playing a diplomatic game of Muslim outreach.

The diplomacy should be left to the State Department and the climate research should be the domain of the Earth scientists.[68]

President Obama has turned NASA into his own private little UN. Needless to say, the folks at NASA are not thrilled with the change of mission from Moon to Muslim.

The former head of NASA on Tuesday described as "deeply flawed" the idea that the space exploration agency's priority should be outreach to Muslim countries, after current Administrator Charles Bolden made that assertion in an interview last month.

"NASA... represents the best of America. Its purpose is not to inspire Muslims or any other cultural entity," Michael Griffin, who served as NASA administrator during the latter half of the Bush administration, told FoxNews.com.[69]

As far as I am concerned the dismantling of our space program in favor Middle East diplomacy is near treason. I live a few miles south of Cape Canaveral where unemployment of many of our brightest prevails while diplomats bow, in the likeness of their President, to Muslims. What happened to Patriotism and American Exceptionalism?

An ungrateful Suffolk University law professor, Michael Avery is offended by students sending care packages to our soldiers in harm's way and is equally offended by an American flag hanging in the college atrium.

A Suffolk University law professor has issued a blistering e-mail calling plans to collect care packages for U.S. troops "shameful." Professor Michael Avery also questioned the intent of an American flag hanging in the law school's atrium. "I think it is shameful that it is perceived as legitimate to solicit in an academic institution for support for men and women who have gone overseas to kill other human beings," Avery wrote in an e-mail to his colleagues. "The United States may well be the most war prone country in the history of civilization." The professor was critical of a program called, "Packages for the Troops." It was an effort within the law school to collect care packages for the nation's military. The e-mail has generated complaints from students and alumni.[70]

Can you imagine the state our country will be in if Progressive Professors like Avery continue pouring their hate of America into our future leader's heads? Avery is a modern day Alinsky brainwashing our youth. Sadly, Professor Avery is not in the minority. Imagine if our borders were overrun sometime in the future and the Federal Government required more than a volunteer army. A call up of troops could happen.

> The draft was ended when the United States military moved to an all-volunteer military force. However, the Selective Service System remains in place as a contingency plan; men between the ages of 18 and 25 are required to register so that a draft can be readily resumed if needed.[71]

How many of our youth today do not think the American Dream is worth defending? How many have been taught that we stand for all things evil? Far too many, of this I am sure.

Professor Avery is a Progressive's Progressive, a law professor, an indoctrinator of our future leaders. He detests our military and the American flag from his podium as he lectures and talks for a living. Suffolk's professor is in need of a reminder from Chuck Colson that our soldiers:

> ...gave up their hopes and dreams, families and friends. They submitted themselves to rigorous discipline...24-hours-a-day duty, and placed their lives in great peril. "Greater love has no one than this that he lays down his life for his friends."

> Their sacrifice ought to inspire in us a profound sense of gratitude. Gratitude for the freedoms we enjoy, bought with a price. And that gratitude should compel us to live lives of service, as well as serving Christ, our neighbor, and yes, our nation.[72]

I cry far too easily, but the following posting on Facebook did me in. It seems a proud US Marine was not allowed to wear his new uniform at his high school graduation.

> Brandon Garabrant graduated from ConVal High School, one day after completing Marine boot camp. His school would not allow Brandon to wear his Marine uniform at graduation...

> CBS Local reported:

> A Marine from New Hampshire has been killed in Afghanistan.

Lance Cpl. Brandon Garabrant, 19, was one of three U.S. service members killed by a roadside bomb Friday morning.

"The entire State of New Hampshire is devastated by the tragic loss of Lance Corporal Brandon Garabrant, who was bravely serving his nation in Afghanistan," Governor Maggie Hassan said in a statement. "Our service men and women courageously sacrifice every day to protect their fellow citizens and defend the enduring value of freedom that is our very core, and in doing so, Lance Corporal Garabrant made the ultimate sacrifice."

Garabrant graduated from ConVal Regional High School in Peterborough last year. He had requested to wear his uniform during graduation, but the school did not allow it.[73]

This posting broke my heart. I have pictured in my mind numerous times young, proud Brandon wanting nothing more than to show off his new uniform. Imagine how honored he was to have graduated from Marine boot camp. Once upon a time, an armed forces uniform would trump a cap and gown. Brandon should have been honored, NOT shunned, for his bravery to volunteer to serve in Afghanistan. As I said, it breaks my heart.

While Brandon breaks my heart, the next article shows just how upside-down our thinking is.

College graduation is a special time in America, and it's even more special this year if you are gay.

A number of public colleges and universities gave special recognition this year to graduating seniors who amazingly managed to complete their degrees while suffering the grueling hardship of being lesbians and homosexuals, reports Campus Reform.

Administrators at these taxpayer-funded institutions allowed gay students to attend this year's commencement ceremonies donning caps and gowns with special honor cords.

Straight students do not appear to have been given the option of having special tassels.

The University of Missouri-Columbia hosted a separate – but equal! – "lavender graduation" for gay students.

"We host Lavender Graduation to honor the accomplishments and hardships members of the LGBTQ and Ally population have had to go through on this campus," explains a description at the website of Mizzou's LGBTQ Resource Center.[74]

What can I say? A special Lavender Graduation. The only reason we have graduations is because of our brave veterans who fought for this great country of ours.

Speaking of upside-down, imagine hanging a flag on your balcony and being asked to take it down because it offended some nearby Muslims. Here is Tran's story.

> WEBSTER, Texas -- A Webster man says his apartment complex manager told him his American flag was a "threat to the Muslim community," and that he has to take it down. But he's not giving up without a fight...

> "What really stunned me is that she said it's a threat towards the Muslim community," said Tran. "I'm not a threat toward anybody."

> We tried to ask a manager if that's exactly what was said, but she just handed us a statement, refused to answer any questions, and called an officer to escort us off the property, before we could press any further:

> > "While the Lodge on El Dorado admires our resident's patriotism, we must enforce our property rules and guidelines. Such guidelines maintain the aesthetics of our apartment community and provide for the safety of all residents. The apartment community already proudly displays our country's flag in a safe and appropriate manner at the entrances to our community."

> But we saw other patriotic symbols hanging from other balconies in the complex, and Tran doesn't plan to budge.

> "I'm gonna leave my flag there, as an American, until she shows me proof that I don't have the right to leave my flag there," said Tran.

> To Tran it's about so much more than stars and stripes.

> "I have friends that died for this country," he said.

> So he says this fight is the least he can do.

We have not heard of any residents complaining about any flags at the complex, or any of the patriotic items we saw. In fact, we spoke to several neighbors who say they want Tran's flag to stay.[75]

It is becoming common for people to fear flying the American flag in fear of offending someone. When I fly to a foreign country, their flag does not offend me in the least. Imagine vacationing in England, Japan or Brazil and asking a national to please take down their flag because of your sensibilities. What is wrong with people?

Then there is our President whose actions seem unbecoming to his role of Commander and Chief. I must admit that I was riveted to my TV when President Obama, speaking from the Rose Garden, announced that a U.S. Soldier had been released in a prisoner swap with the Taliban in Afghanistan. Few details were known at the time but when our President turned the microphone over to a thankful father, I nearly threw a book at my TV screen.

Appearing with President Obama in a brief Rose Garden event, Robert Bergdahl, the father of Army Sgt. Bowe Bergdahl, recited "Bismillah ir-Rahman ir-Rahm," according to the Daily Caller. In English, that means, "In the name of Allah, most Gracious, most Compassionate."

When he finished reciting, the president hugged him.

Bergdahl's words echoed the Taliban's official reaction to the prisoner swap. In a statement, the group that has been at war with the United States since 2001 announced that five of its members who had been held at the American prison at Guantanamo Bay prison had been released, "due to the benevolence of Allah Almighty and the sacrifices of the heroic and courageous Mujahadin of the Islamic Emirate."

Bergdahl's use of a Muslim prayer and the Taliban's portrayal of it as a clear victory for their movement – Taliban leader Mullah Omar on Sunday called the release from Gitmo a "big win" in the Pakistani news outlet Dawn.com – is sure to increase the controversy around Obama's prisoner swap, helped by a tweet posted to Berdahl's Twitter account last week vowing to work for the release of the rest of the prisoners at the prison. (That tweet has been deleted.)[76]

Until recently our government took the hard like position that "we do not negotiate with terrorists." To add insult-to-injury the President effected the exchange without the mandatory notifications to the House and the Senate. Our President broke the law again. Marching to Alinsky's drum, President Obama took from *Rules for Radicals;* "Ethical standards must be elastic to stretch with the times." Pg. 30/31. You see, you can't really deal fairly, truthfully or morally with a Progressive because he or she only lives by rules which they feel free to massage *whenever* the need arises.

How heart wrenching and maddening is this from a grieving Mother?

Diane Foley, mother of beheaded journalist James Foley, said she was 'embarrassed and appalled' by the Obama administration

In an interview with CNN, the grieving mother said officials told her family they could be prosecuted if they tried to raise a ransom to free her son. They were also told the U.S. would not exchange prisoners or carry out a military action to try and rescue James Foley, she said. She knocked the Obama administration for its inaction…

…Diane Foley said government officials told her family they could face legal action if they tried to raise a ransom to free her son from his ISIS captors.

Officials said it "was illegal (and) we might be prosecuted," Foley told CNN.

New Hampshire native James Foley, 40, was kidnapped by ISIS terrorists in November 2012 while reporting from Syria. He was executed by an ISIS militant, whose cowardly face was hooded, on Aug. 19, with the grisly footage posted online.

"I think our efforts to get Jim freed were an annoyance," Foley told CNN's Anderson Cooper Thursday night.

"It didn't seem to be in (U.S.) strategic interest, if you will," she said.

The devastated parent told Cooper that Foley family members were warned not to go to the media. They were also told the U.S. would not exchange prisoners or carry out a military action to rescue the captured journalist.

"Jim would have been saddened" by the U.S. response, she told Cooper. "Jim believed, till the end, that his country would come to (his) aid. Our country let Jim down.[77]

America did let Jim Foley down. The priorities of this administration are incredibly misplaced. Our Secretary of State is worrying about expanding his base of LGBT diplomats while our citizens are being beheaded.

Here is another example of revisionist hypocrisy i.e. the double standard of the "ends justifies the means."

It is amazing how politicians see things when their party is in power as opposed to how they see them when they are not in power. When George Bush was the president, Congress gave him authority to use military force and about three of the nearly twenty items dealt with weapons of mass destruction (WMD). When it was reported that no WMD were found and when the war in Iraq was in chaos liberals started talking about Bush's illegal war and that he overstepped his authority.

Fast forward to now. Barack Obama has made a mess of Iraq and his "greatest achievement" is falling apart as terrorists slice through that country like Hitler through Europe. He is considering military action in Iraq and Nancy Pelosi has indicated that he does not need to come to Congress for approval because the authorities are already there as a result of the 2001 and 2003 legislation that Bush used to engage in Iraq.

Pelosi told reporters that she agreed that the president has all of the authorities that he needs in the authorizations to use military force passed by Congress previously.

"All of the authorities are there. That doesn't mean I want all of them to be used, especially boots on the ground," she said. "But I definitely think the president has all of the authority he needs by dint of legislation that was passed in 2001 and 2003."

She appeared to be referring to the authorizations to use military force passed after the Sept. 11, 2001 attacks and the 2002 authorization to use force in Iraq. Neither of those authorizations have [sic] expired, although the official White House position is that the Iraq authorization should be repealed.

Obama is using, and Pelosi is supporting, the authorizations that the White House thinks should be repealed.

In other words, Pelosi and her liberal pals all said Bush did not have the authority to do what he did but that Obama has the authority, under the same legislation, to do what Bush did even though Obama thinks the authorization should be repealed.

This is how liberals think. They gave Bush authority and then said he abused it but now that Obama is doing the very same thing (or considering doing it) they say he has the authority.[78]

It's as the old saying goes, repeat something often enough and it will be believed. Something like, "Hope and Change."

Attack by Overreach

What is the job description of the Secretary of State? The website defines the department's responsibilities in detail should you desire further study at http://www.state.gov/secretary/115194.htm.

Often it looks as if the job description should really read; "...fighting to bring justice to this mean, unfair, unjust, racist, bigoted, homophobic country...we have the rise of the demographic shift where social justice and tolerance are the definitions of the new America."[79] With all the upheaval going on in the world today, John Kerry is making more headway with lesbian, bisexual and transgender issues than he is with foreign ones.

With much of the Obama administration's foreign policy in tatters, John Kerry is clear on at least one goal he hopes to achieve by the end of his time as secretary of state: having lesbian, bisexual, and transgender ambassadors representing the United States. In remarks to a GLIFAA (formerly Gays and Lesbians in Foreign Affairs Agencies) Pride event in the Ben Franklin Room at the State Department, the secretary ran through a litany of accomplishments by the Obama administration that benefit the "LGBT/gay community." During his speech, Kerry said that, if confirmed, Ted Osius (nominated by President Obama for the post in Vietnam) would be the sixth openly gay U.S. ambassador currently in service:

> So I am very proud of the progress that we are now making even in appointing LGBT ambassadors. I worked with the committee here at the State Department – with the D Committee, and I worked with the White House. And as a result, Ted Osius, sitting here, whom I've known a long time, and his family I know, will be the first openly LGBT officer nominated to serve as an ambassador in Asia. And on confirmation, he's going to join five openly gay ambassadors who are now serving their country. I'm working hard to ensure that by the end of my tenure, we will have lesbian, bisexual, and transgender ambassadors in our ranks as well.[80]

Kerry went on to elaborate about a transgender Foreign Service Officer who had a tough time being accepted at her post in Bucharest. Kerry proudly proclaimed;

> In the end, she won the hearts of the Ambassador, her career Foreign Service colleagues, Civil Service colleagues, and the local staff, and she actually made Embassy Bucharest a model of acceptance. She even authored the first State Department report on transgender issues, and she didn't just get through a difficult period, she was determined to turn it into a precedent-setting event, and as a result she made it a lot easier for those – or at least a little easier for those who follow.[81]

Let's disregard foreign affairs issues. We have bigger more important fish to fry. We have transgender issues to deal with! According to the Williams Institute review conducted in April 2011, approximately 0.03% of the American population is transgender.[82] Kerry plans to take a firm stand against foreign countries which do not embrace the Obama administration"s progressive policies: "...we are instructing our embassies to inform governments locally that this is our policy and that they need to honor our policy. It's that simple."[83] Yep, it's that simple. All foreign governments should drop dead over Kerry's preferred 0.03% of America. Let's see how well that works for gays and transsexual diplomats assigned to Muslim countries.

Not only are the President and his Cabinet overreaching, but the First Lady has thrown her hat into the ring. Once again, the Progressives know more than parents and stand ready to take the helm. It seems that although Michelle Obama was educated at Princeton and Harvard she required counseling on how to feed her two girls in a healthy manner. I am quite confident our Framers did not anticipate powerful First Ladies pushing big government. Here is a blurb about our First Lady at work:

> In an interview with MSN's Healthy Living, she made two particular statements that deserve further comment.
>
> *Before coming to the White House, I struggled, as a working parent with a traveling, busy husband, to figure out how to feed my kids healthy, and I didn't get it right.*
>
> *Our pediatrician had to pull me aside and point out some things that were going wrong.*
>
> *I thought to myself, if a Princeton and Harvard educated professional woman doesn't know how to adequately feed her kids, then what are other parents going through who don't have access to the information I have?*[84]

Really! With a family income of nearly one half million dollars a year, Michelle and then Senator Barak Obama required a pediatrician to instruct them on eating right. They have numerous academic degrees but not a lick of good old common sense. Perhaps her story is really a Progressive set up for a more powerful Federal Government. "It's so important for our schools to make the hard calls for our kids, because parents are struggling enough at home." Parents truly are making the "hard calls" when it comes to their children or - should be. Michelle's government Choose**MyPlate**.gov meal plan is yet another example of the government taking, yes taking, more and more control over our lives. For the most part our schools are better run by mothers and fathers of students than Michelle and Barack and a bunch of condescending bureaucrats. Perhaps Princeton and Harvard should offer nutrition classes to students who feel they can run the country but require assistance understanding the basic food groups no matter the configuration de jour. I have provided for you the latest and greatest from Choose**MyPlate**.gov.

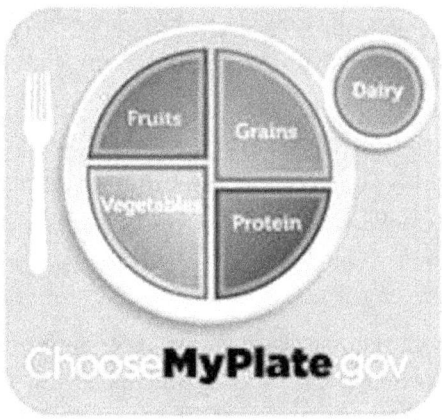

Isn't it remarkable how little has changed?

Taking the school meal programs a step further we have schools deciding who is overweight and who is not. We all know New York and California are the cutting edge Nanny States but New York City has outdone itself. "Gwendolyn Williams is a pencil-thin, bubbly 9-year-old who is a perfectly healthy third-grader. But according to city bureaucrats, she's practically obese."[85] Gwendolyn lives in Staten Island and received a Department of Education "Fitnessgram" that described her BMI (body mass index) as "overweight." "'I'm 4-foot-1, and 66 pounds, and I'm like, what?!' Gwendolyn exclaimed of the school handout, which the city is sending home in the bookbags of 870,000 public school students, grades K through 12."[86] The Fitnessgram was to have been sealed, but the position of the seal allowed young Gwendolyn to read the message. Gwendolyn asked her mom about the note and if her thighs were too overweight. Needless to say, it broke the stay-at-home mom's heart. Fitnessgrams have gone over like a lead balloon. "'Fat-shaming,' experts called the practice on Thursday, criticizing both the fallibility of BMI calculations and the mental-health effects of kids being graded on their size."[87]

BMI, while supported by the federal Centers for Disease Control and Prevention, was designed decades ago by the insurance industry as a way of assessing the health of groups of people, not individuals, said Chevese Turner of the Binge Eating Disorder Association.

Dieting, especially for kids, is the gateway drug for eating disorders, and so is the public shaming that can come with this," she said of the Fitnessgrams.

"My organization and others believe that BMI report cards have no place coming from schools and can be more harmful than helpful."

A DOE spokeswoman defended the Fitnessgrams Thursday as just one indicator ... "which helps students develop personal goals for life-long health."[88]

How much hard earned tax payer money goes into projects such as this? I submit if New Yorkers had ANY say as to how their money is spent, they would overwhelmingly prefer the subways be updated and the roads rid of nasty pot-holes. Come on, no amount of Fitnessgrams or legislation is going to fix obesity.

PART II

THE PROGRESSIVE ATTACK ON CAPITALISM

4

CAPITALISM

Free market

"If governments or central banks really can create wealth simply by creating money,
why does poverty exist anywhere on earth?"
Ron Paul

Let's get one thing straight: Socialists and Progressives loathe Capitalism because it minimizes the role of government and maximizes the role of the individual. Socialists and Progressives prefer Socialism: "a way of organizing a society in which major industries are owned and controlled by the government rather than by individual people and companies." It is an uphill battle for free enterprise types, like our Founders, as ever expanding-government wears away and weakens private enterprise. Innovation is part of America's DNA and must be allowed to thrive if we are to remain the innovators we have proven ourselves to be.

Many prominent economists believe the seemingly unrestricted printing of money is sure to bring about inflation that will greatly harm many Americans. Increasing the money supply (printing money), increases the price of goods and services because inflation causes the value of the dollar to go down. Suppose you collect comic books and one day the publisher decides to print thousands and thousands of new editions in order to better his standard of living. The more new comic books that are printed, the less valuable your copy becomes.

> Forbes.com contributor Eamonn Fingleton has envisioned such a doomsday scenario. Quoting economist Paul Craig Roberts, he writes that the collapse of the dollar could create an apocalyptic situation to which "shoppers at Walmart will feel like they are shopping at Neiman Marcus.[89]

You will understand how powerful and persuasive Fingleton's analogy is if you ever have an opportunity to shop at Nieman's.

Our Founding Fathers set the standard for anticipating and planning for problems the Republic might encounter years after they were laid to rest. I imagine they stayed up many long nights strategically planning and "what if-ing," should, this, that, or the other occur. It probably never crossed their minds that Americans would one day cast their vote to favor leaders espousing a serf or bondage system. Dinesh D'Souza explains the American serf.

> Consider this startling fact. While the top 1 percent of Americas pay more than one-third of all federal income taxes, and the next 9 percent pays another third, the bottom 50 percent of Americans pays no federal income tax at all. This is grossly unfair. Obama is right about the unfairness of the system. In reality it is unfair to the successful![90]

America did not invent Capitalism but America does Capitalism like no one else.

> The "spirit of capitalism," it has been alleged, was extant among merchants as far back as the fourteenth and the fifteenth centuries, and a private attitude toward certain categories of business pursuits could be discovered in the writings of the Scholastics.[91]

Modern Capitalism is heavily rooted in Adam Smith's book *Wealth of Nations* first published in 1776. It once served as a guide for America's economic policies. It was required reading when I studied economics and remains a classic. "So profound was the impact of *Wealth of Nations* that it is generally considered the most important economic work ever written. Terms that are commonly used today, such as "invisible hand" and "division of labor," had their genesis in Smith's treatise."[92] Adam Smith is known as the Founder of Capitalism.

> One of Smith's initial observations was that production was enhanced by the assigning of specific tasks to individual workers. This division of labor would maximize production by allowing workers to specialize in discrete aspects of the production process. He saw in the division of labor and in expanding markets virtually limitless possibilities for the expansion of wealth through manufacture and trade.

> Smith also argued that capital for the production and distribution of wealth could work most effectively in the absence of government interference. Such a laissez-faire—that is, "leave alone" or "allow to be"—policy (a term popularized by *The Wealth of Nations*) would, in his opinion, encourage the most efficient operation of private and commercial enterprises. He was not against government involvement in public projects too large for private investment, but rather objected to its meddling in the market mechanism.

> He also held that individuals acting in their own self-interest would naturally seek out economic activities that provided the greatest financial rewards. Smith was convinced that this self-interest would in turn maximize the economic well-being of society as a whole...[93]

Adam Smith believed that free trade was the opposite of war and in many ways he has proven to be prophetic. Philosophers, back in the day, debated how to harness negative passions into virtues;

> ...the ides of engineering social progress by cleverly setting up one passion to fight another became a fairly common intellectual pastime in the course of the eighteenth century. It is indeed expressed by a host of writers, minor as well as major, in general or applied form.[94]

Counteracting the passions became a major point of debate. "From France to England the idea traveled to America where it was used by the Founding

Fathers as an important intellectual tool for the purposes of constitutional engineering."[95]

The concept is really quite fundamental: if men are working and trading they are not warring. Trade is a good thing despite what you hear from many. "The fact that the United States buys products and services from other nations doesn't mean it is weak; it means that the U.S. economy is strong and has the wealth and resources to buy what others are selling."[96] Below are a few outstanding quotes…

> Scottish historian William Robertson, who writes in his *View of the Progress of Society in Europe* (1769): Commerce tends to wear off prejudices which maintain distinctions and animosity between nations. It *softens and polishes* the manners of men.[97]

> Montesquieu – "the natural effect of commerce is to lead to peace. Two nations that trade together become mutually dependent: if one has an interest in buying, the other has one in selling; and all unions are based on mutual needs."[98]

Capitalism is more efficient than Socialism but Capitalism without Christianity is no better than Socialism. The Founders strongly believed a free market system would serve the newly founded Republic best. A free market system is "… an economic system that allows supply and demand to regulate prices, wages, etc., rather than government policy."[99] The Founders' vision produced unprecedented results":

> The United States of America or USA has long been the global superpower in terms of economic prosperity and technological advancement for some decades now. Accounting for only 5% of the world's population, it produces more than one fourth of the global economic output.[100]

The Framers knew the more merchants and middle class workers, the more stable the Republic would be. If Adam Smith had his way, he would bar interference of government in the affairs of commerce.

> Following the example of Great Britain, Alexander Hamilton established the First Bank of the United States, as well as a mint with a dollar fixed by law to a specific weight in gold. Hamilton's system of banking

and stable money quickly attracted and generated capital. It turned the American economy into the leading industrial power in the world."[101]

Hamilton knew that stability was key as only a stable base will hold over the long haul. Both entrepreneurs and workers are drawn to stability. Aren't we all! All will invest and work longer and harder when they feel their future is secure. To maintain a free market, it is obvious that individual freedom is a necessity. "To put it simply, Smith believed that the "general (material) welfare is best served by letting each member of society pursue his own (material) self-interest."[102]

Part and parcel of a free market are also risk and reward. When I started a business in New York, I put my savings on the line knowing full well and accepting the fact that I risked my entire net worth. While the downside was risk, the upside was reward more commonly known as "profit." Opening a small business was the most time-consuming, difficult and exhausting challenge I ever took on, but it paid off. Today, especially in liberal states like New York and California, I would no longer contemplate opening a business due to the lack of market stability and governmental overreach. It is incredibly more difficult, costlier and riskier to open a business today than in the past for a myriad of reasons. The paperwork alone is enough to scare most away.

My business was a partnership. Today there would be a mandated third partner looming overhead – the government. It took us months to obtain the necessary sign permits for our Real Estate office on North Bellmore, Long Island. Over the years, the town made a fortune from our building signage not to mention the numerous yard signs our agents placed on their listings front lawns. Sign permits are not cheap and must be renewed by the town every so often. It seemed that everything we touched had some sort of business fee attached. When a candidate for "judge" asked to place a very large sign on our businesses front lawn, we asked if she had the necessary sign permits as we did not want a summons calling us to court. She responded as she chuckled, "Not to worry, we voted our election signage exempt from the town rules and fees you have to pay!" Our Framers must be spinning in their graves. Small business owners are made to jump through hoops to procure expensive permits while the politicians exempted themselves. Note that near-bankrupt states are setting up free enterprise zones to attract businesses. It is too bad it took everyone going broke for these states to figure out Socialism does not work. Isn't it common sense that people will flee from high-taxed and ill-maintained towns and states to lower-taxed and better-maintained towns and states taking their businesses and resources with them? It's human nature!

Like small town bureaucrats, Congress has exempted itself from the Affordable Care Act (ACA – AKA ObamaCare.) The poor taxpayer is at the mercy of a bill voted into law without being read.

ObamaCare is a bureaucratic dream come true. It involves more departments and agencies than you can imagine:

> ...requires substantial coordination between multiple government agencies with very different infrastructures. As the GAO notes, the data hub is to verify an applicant's Social Security number with the Social Security Administration (SSA), and to access the data from the Internal Revenue Service (IRS) and the Department of Homeland Security (DHS) that are needed to assess the applicant's income, citizenship, and immigration status. The data hub is also expected to access information from the Veterans Health Administration (VHA), Department of Defense (DOD), Office of Personnel Management (OPM), and Peace Corps to enable exchanges to determine if an applicant is eligible for insurance coverage from other federal programs that would make them ineligible for income-based financial subsidies.

> But that's not all. The website then needs to match this data from multiple government agencies with the various policy offerings of multiple private insurers with multiple offerings, each with their own computer system and rates.[103]

ObamaCare is how our government set about simplifying the health care system. I can't imagine a bunch of bureaucrats attempting to simplify anything. Many predict that the ACA may collapse under its own bureaucratic weight.

Capitalism in the United States for the last 200 years has been quite a success story. It is the story of the sharpest minds leading the way through innovation and hard work. Economic scholar Ludwig von Mises sums up the history of Capitalism like few can.

The history of capitalism as it has operated in the last two hundred years in the realm of Western civilization is the record of a steady rise in the wage earners' standard of living. The inherent mark of capitalism is that it is mass production for mass consumption directed by the most energetic and far-sighted individuals, unflaggingly aiming at improvement. Its driving force is the profit motive, the instrumentality of which forces the businessman constantly to provide the consumers with more, better, and cheaper amenities. An excess of profits over losses can appear only in a progressing economy and only to the extent to which the masses' standard of living improves. Thus capitalism is the system under which the keenest and most agile minds are driven to promote to the best of their abilities the welfare of the laggard many.

In the field of historical experience it is impossible to resort to measurement. As money is no yardstick of value and want satisfaction, it cannot be applied for comparing the standard of living of people in various periods of time. However, all historians whose judgment is not muddled by romantic prepossessions agree that the evolution of capitalism has multiplied capital equipment on a scale which far exceeded the synchronous increase in population figures. Capital equipment both per capita of the total population and per capita of those able to work is immensely larger today than fifty, a hundred, or two hundred years ago. Concomitantly there has been a tremendous increase in the quota the wage earners receive out of the total amount of commodities produced, an amount that in itself is much bigger than in the past.

The ensuing rise in the masses' standard of living is miraculous when compared with the conditions of ages gone by. In those merry old days, even the wealthiest people led an existence that must be called straightened when compared with the average standard of the American or Australian worker of our age. Capitalism, says Marx, unthinkingly repeating the fables of the eulogists of the Middle Ages, has an inevitable tendency to impoverish the workers more and more. The truth is that capitalism has poured a horn of plenty upon the masses of wage earners, who frequently did all they could to sabotage the adoption of those innovations that render their life more agreeable. How uneasy an American worker would be if he were forced to live in the manor of a medieval lord and to miss the plumbing facilities and the other gadgets he simply takes for granted![104]

In a free market economy, such as ours, supply and demand determines which goods and/or services will thrive and which will fail. A market is no longer free when a bunch of bureaucrats in Washington D.C., with agenda-driven hands, are the determining factor of what goods will line the shelves of your local grocery store or what services are offered around town. The hand governing the marketplace should be "invisible," thereby fairly allocating and fairly distributing the country's output.

Under the optimal condition of market efficiency, the price of a commodity is said to be unique at which the seller wants to sell the product simultaneously equals the price which the buyer wants to pay for the product. Markets allow transactions to be decentralized to the level where decisions made by the producers and consumers adjust the system into equilibrium.[105]

To put it simply, demand by buyers, instead of government committees or executive orders ought to drive the market.

When a marketplace is unencumbered by governmental intervention and is free to call the shots the results can be stunning as innovation is unleashed. Innovation is what made the American economic system great. While agricultures share of the Gross National Product has declined, the technological share of GNP is off the charts. "With technological superiority in the field of computers, aerospace and military equipment, the country now boasts of one of the highest per capita incomes in the world."[106] What comes to mind when you think of innovation?

One prime example is the explosive boom of Silicon Valley startups out of the Stanford Industrial Park. In 1957, dissatisfied employees of Shockley Semiconductor, the company of Nobel laureate and co-inventor of the transistor William Shockley, left to form an independent firm, Fairchild Semiconductor. After several years, Fairchild developed into a formidable presence in the sector. Eventually, these founders left to start their own companies based on their own, unique, latest ideas, and then leading employees started their own firms. Over the next 20 years, this snowball process launched the momentous startup company explosion of information technology firms. Essentially, Silicon Valley began as 65 new enterprises born out of Shockley's eight former employees.[107]

Relative Poverty

The Progressive plan is to separate effort from reward. Their goal is to spread the countries proceeds around to cover everyone as fairly as big government defines fair. "Earned wealth belongs to everyone in the community and "the government has every right to seize it and distribute it however it wants."[108] The distribution of one worker's money or goods to another is what the Progressives call "fair share." It may seem fair to the recipient, but to the forced donor there is often a sting of not-so-fair.

Something like this has happened to America in the past few decades. In the period following World War II, most Americans were middle-class. There was a small number-say 10 percent-of poor people and a small number-say 5 percent-of rich people. Today the fraction for the poor is about the same, although the poor live much better that they used to. At one time America had the kind of poverty we see in developing nations. Economists call it "absolute poverty." In America today, there is virtually no absolute poverty; there is only relative poverty. Indeed poor people in America have a standard of living that is higher than 75 percent of the world's population. Not only are our poor better housed, better clothed, and better fed than average Americans were in the first half of the twentieth century, but in some respects-including the size of their living space-they live better than the average European today. Our poor have automobiles, TV sets, microwave ovens, central heat and cell phones.[109]

The quote from above bears repeating:

Indeed poor people in America have a standard of living that is higher than 75 percent of the world's population. Not only are our poor better housed, better clothed, and better fed than average Americans were in the first half of the twentieth century, but in some respects-including the size of their living space-they live better than the average European today. Our poor have automobiles, TV sets, microwave ovens, central heat and cell phones.[110]

America is blessed. Think about it, if the Progressives get their way and create a borderless world with equalized wealth, then even America's 5% poor will have less. I am beginning to understand why the Progressives idolize Europe as I learn more and more of their worldview.

OPM - Other People's Money

We all know government is inefficient. Inefficiency is built into the system as it stands today. Washington, D.C. has the luxury of spending other people's hard-earned tax dollars with little accountability. They do not share the concerns of business owners as their life savings and personal residences are not on the line. Washington, D.C. gets to play with OPM and need not be concerned with trivialities such as competition, cost, regulatory constraints, taxes or profit and loss statements, etc. Imagine running a business without having to concern yourself with bouncing a check. When the bottom line is no longer a consideration, then all sorts of inefficiencies such as featherbedding and incompetency not to mention cronyism creep into play. I remind you that Congress has exempted itself and its cronies from the Affordable Care Act. Most representatives in Washington, D.C. believe they are smarter than the average middle class worker or small business owner and scheme to protect us by creating a Nanny State, where they are the CEO, COO, Treasurer etc. In other words, they would be in total control of just about everything. If the Progressives were to lose office and Fiscal Conservatives were to succeed in downsizing the bureaucracy, some of the bureaucrats would have to work for a living – hold down and an actual job. Imagine that!

When I was the Director of Cargo Sales for Pan American Airways, I had the pleasure of dining with the then Postmaster General William F. Bolger. During our luncheon, sometime in the 70's, he announced that he was going to streamline the Postal Service to ensure its bottom line. Postmaster General Bolger said they were going to stop Saturday delivery as well as force all new construction to build postal centers comprised of post office boxes at the end of the block or entrance of the development. When I retired, over twenty years after our luncheon, and moved to Florida, the new construction I purchased had a postbox placed in the front yard as do the yards of all my neighbors. I mention this because I ran across the following article not too long ago which points out the futility of Washington, D.C.

> A House committee has approved a proposal that would end door-to-door mail delivery for millions of Americans in favor of communal or curbside boxes.

> The House Oversight and Government Reform Committee approved the measure on an 18-13 party-line vote Wednesday. The bill would direct the U.S. Postal Service to convert 15 million addresses over the next decade to the less costly, but also less convenient delivery method...

> The Postal Service reported a $1.9 billion loss for the first three months this year despite continued cost-cutting, a 2.3 percent rise in operating revenue and increased employee productivity. Package business has risen but the service continues to struggle with inflationary cost increases and a continued decline in first-class mailing as people move to the Internet for letter writing and bill paying.[111]

Last week I asked my local postman if Saturday delivery was going to end. He look at me and laughed stating, "Are you kidding? The Post Office is a cash cow for Washington." My postman drove away in his nifty little Jeep cracking up over my question. You know what, he probably is correct. Nothing, absolutely nothing, has changed since our luncheon in the 70's. Why should it now? The Post Office is still hawking the same tired old plan dating back to pre-email, cell phones, texting, etc. It is pitiful!

Here are a few ways the Progressives we voted into office are taking care of us:

Louisiana Legislators Vote to Exempt Themselves from Gun Ban...

...The bill allows lawmakers to carry concealed weapons inside public buildings, except the State Capitol. If you're just a regular citizen, even with a concealed carry permit, you're not allowed.[112]

To ensure they stay in office, the rules seem to be massageable. I could not agree with the NY Daily News more.

News broke earlier this month that the second-longest serving member of the House of Representatives would not be able to run for reelection after failing to obtain the required number of signatures on his nominating petitions. In fact, he had less than half of those required.

But the man in question, John Conyers, Jr., a Democrat representing the Detroit area, has proven that rules were meant to be broken, because a federal judge has just decided that Conyers will be allowed to be on the Democratic primary ballot in August, according to NY Daily News. The decision came hours after Michigan's Secretary of State declined to put him on the ballot.

Regardless of Conyers' party, he didn't follow the rules, and should not be on the ballot. This is the perfect example of why the American public has a deep distrust of politicians and the political process – those in power will lie, cheat, and steal to stay there![113]

Changes on the Horizon

I was taught by my parents to work hard and smart and if I did then things would flow my way (I would be rewarded.) Today, the government is raising (notice I said government not parents,) a generation that believes it is totally acceptable to return and live in mom's and dad's basement confident goods and services (their "fair share") will flow their way. Should they fall short of cash, there are always mom's and dad's pension fund to draw from or home to mortgage. To many, the government and their parents are viewed as ATM's.

I love reading Christian fiction especially, when the plot deals with cultural issues that challenge us all. While reading Randy Alcorn's *The Ishbane Conspiracy*, I came across a quote that at first amused me then saddened me greatly. Half of the book is about demons whose sole reason for being is to constantly place roadblocks between our youth and their Creator. The conspiracy is working and the Devil boasts…

> This generation has been given more and less than any other. More wealth, recreation, technology, and free time. Less morals, guidance, discipline and inspiration. They've been coddled and patronized. Bought off in exchange for their passivity. Parents smothering their children with toys and technology is my favorite kind of child abuse. The more they have, the less they enjoy. The more activities thrust upon them, the more they're bored.[114]

Alcorn and company are quite correct in that our youth are on a treadmill to disaster. Someone is going to have to explain to them that they are not going to have all the stuff their parents have like big homes and state-of-the-art cars, etc. Who is going to take the blame? We adults will one day be forced to man-up and woman-up and admit we allowed liberal college professors to brainwash our children who now embrace their liberal thinking. Shame on us as many voted for candidates promising "free" medical care or "free" birth control pills knowing full well NOTHING is free. To some, Obama's actions are viewed as manna from heaven while others feel plundered, robbed, pillaged, looted etc. You get what you vote for. Or you get what others vote for when you stay at home and pout like many Evangelicals did in 2012. Capitalism versus Socialism are two points of view as wide apart as Progressives can possible stretch the chiasm. The Progressive chiasm alienates Americans one from another or to put it in Progressive speak, the "have and the have-nots."

The Wall Street Journal Sunday of June 29, 2014 outlines some very interesting facts about Gen-Xers – those born between 1965 and 1980. The article by Quentin Fottrell is an eye opener. America's Gen-Xers were just beginning to work when they were hit with everything from the tech crash to 9/11 and today's economy. Fottrell points out:

…by most measures Gen Xers are worse off financially than earlier generations. As of 2010, Gen Xers' assets were only double their debts, according to the Pew Charitable Trusts. By contrast, the "Silent Generation" (people born during the Depression and World War II) had assets 27 times their debts, while older baby boomers' assets were about four times their debt.

Starting life with higher student-debt loads than their elders made it harder for Gen-Xers to get financially established. A leveling-off of U.S. incomes has also hurt them. "In the U.S. the expectation is that every generation does better than the last one, but this has not been the case for Generation X," says Signe-Mary McKernan, senior fellow and economist at the Urban Institute.

The Millennial generation born in the early 1980s to the early 2000s followed the Gen-Xers. They are unique as they are very self-asserting and want what they want. Jessica White of *The Columbus Dispatch* wrote a fascinating article about the Millenials.

They've been painted by some as lazy and entitled and can come off as smartphone-addicted know-it-alls to their bosses.

They might demand their dream job coming out of college, reluctant to follow their parents' path of starting off small and working their way up.

And the unemployment rate for millennials — spanning ages 18 to early 30s — remains well above that of other age groups.

Are millennials their own biggest enemy when it comes to getting their careers off the ground?

Some observers say that's possible.

Many of these stereotypes are not new; older generations have complained about younger ones for years, said Jamie Gutfreund of Los Angeles-based Intelligence Group, which studies generational trends.

But thanks to technology and new societal influences, the complainers might have a point. Millennials have a unique attitude about work that doesn't quite fit the workforce — but that might not be a bad thing.

Gutfreund studies the differing motivations and preferences of the generations. A member of Generation X, she said Xers — ages mid-30s through late 40s — were culturally different from the baby-boom generation before them.

While boomers insisted on being heard by the world, Xers were a smaller generation who felt they had to fight to have a voice, she said.

"Millennials were raised with a different perspective," she said. "Their boomer parents taught them to believe their opinions are important."

Older generations view the boss as an expert whose attention must be earned. But because of social media, where celebrities and moguls are just a tweet away, millennials think they can go in on their first day and share ideas with the CEO.

And if a manager asks a millennial employee to jump, the employee is more likely to ask, " Why?..."

...Millennials also want to find purpose in their career, Gutfreund said, which might not mean having the highest pay.

"They want to make meaning, not just money," she said.

In a recent Intelligence Group study, 64 percent of millennials said they would rather make $40,000 a year at a job they love than $100,000 a year at a job they think is boring.

It's admirable, Gutfreund said, but it also can cause frustration when a millennial is forced to work somewhere unfulfilling, and it might mean skipping entry-level jobs that could lead to something better.

When you ask millennials where they'd like to work, the answer is generally Google, Apple or freelancing or for themselves, Gutfreund said. They tend to be flexible, unstructured and nonlinear, which can be misunderstood by structured, 9-to-5 office managers...

"They're not a hierarchical generation," Gutfreund said. "They're incredibly collaborative, and they're moving into a workforce that is not ready for them.[115]

I find it interesting that by the year "2020 they'll comprise more than a third of adults or that by 2025 they could make up 75% or more of the workforce."[116] Just think of the impact.

Brookings Institute researchers Morley Winograd and Dr. Michael Hais write that millennials' attitudes towards work, commerce, and governance are fundamentally different enough from preceding generations that "the force of the changes they are capable of creating is beginning to be felt in all sectors of America's economy." Given both their swelling number and radically different priorities, millennials are poised to fundamentally rewrite the way the economy functions. It will not be good for business-as-usual and give rise to new industries and priorities.[117]

Tom McKay of policymic.com goes on to say that 88 percent of Millennials do their banking online and 50 percent do their banking with their smartphones. Millennials do not think like Boomers as they value increased regulation. They have listened well to their liberal college professors. They will create change like we have never seen before as they are the most diverse, networked and free-thinking generation in our history.

If Hillary Clinton runs for President in two years, she might have luck with a younger crowd.

A new survey shows that 39% of millennials registered to vote would cast their ballot for the former secretary of state if she won the Democratic nomination, according to libertarian-leaning poll conductor Reason-Rupe.

Coming in second was first-term Massachusetts Sen. Elizabeth Warren, whom 8% said they would vote for if she runs for President in two years, according to the poll. The progressive legislator would fare just better than Vice President Joe Biden, with 6% saying they would support him.

Representative Paul Ryan, the 2012 Republican Vice Presidential candidate, did the best among GOP potentials with 6%.

One thing, however, was consistent among the 2,000 surveyed, regardless of political party identification — a majority has lost faith in the government.

About two-thirds of those polled — all of whom were ages 18 to 29 — said they think the U.S. government is "inefficient and wasteful" — a 24-percentage-point jump from when Reason-Rupe did the survey five years ago...

...they favor more progressive policies with 71% supporting a $10.10 an hour minimum wage hike, according to the poll.[118]

Boomers like Roger and myself were born post WWII between 1946 and 1964. Boomers are the generation that received peak incomes and took advantage of an abundance of goods and services. We have consumed like none that went before us, and as a result, have placed the future of our children and grandchildren at risk. Add to this a Progressive President printing money almost as fast as he can spend it and inherences may be a thing of the past. To add insult to injury, many Boomers have not sufficiently funded their retirement. Wikipedia .org states...

> 60% lost value in investments because of the economic crisis.
>
> 42% are delaying retirement.
>
> 25% claim they'll never retire.

Serfing America

We titled our book *Serfing America* because that is precisely what the Progressives are doing to the middle class. A serf is a worker who is allowed to keep some of the fruits of his labor. A serf was far worse off than our Founders' vision of a laissez-faire worker in America. Laissez-faire is "a doctrine opposing governmental interference in economic affairs beyond the minimum necessary for the maintenance of peace and property rights."[119]

> Karl Marx points out that "the peasant serf...worked three days for himself on his own field or the field allotted to him, and the three subsequent days he performed compulsory and gratuitous labor on the estate of his lord." Marx appreciated the clarity of the system: "here the paid and unpaid part of labor were sensibly separated." So at least the serf could realize the degree to which he was being ripped off. And the thieves were the lords and aristocrats, who lived off the labor of the serfs. The serf worked, and they ate.

> America's tax rates, we may recall with some surprise, impose basically the same terms on successful citizens as those imposed on the medieval serf. The top federal rate is nearly 40 percent, and with other

taxes piled on, the top rate easily reaches 50 percent. What this means is that half of the labor of these citizens is confiscated up front; another way to look at it is that the first half of the year they work for the government, and only the second half of the year they work for themselves and their families.[120]

The Nanny State is not only overseeing the equalization of assets; they are making assets harder to realize. The amount of regulation imposed on businesses is oppressive and is a disincentive. The Affordable Care Act is a regulatory nightmare which, as mentioned before, our leaders have exempted themselves and many of their major contributors from. Washington, D.C. fancies itself as wise and a lot like Robin Hood overseeing Sherwood Forest (bailouts.) Sadly, often it is robbing from shareholders which in many cases come down to robbing from middle class retirement accounts. Obama and his ilk are most certainly not Robin Hood. They are simply robbers!

Forbes

My favorite economist is Steve Forbes. I describe his school of thought as one based on history; what has and has not worked in the past. He is a master of common sense and has the ability to make the complex read easy. His bestselling book, *Money: How the Destruction of the Dollar Threatens the Global Economy-and What We Can Do About It*, is an educational as well as provocative read. It is a wake up call for anyone with assets. The book kicks off with an in-depth look at the history of the dollar including our departure from the gold standard. It is fascinating and tragic how much has changed since Nixon's infamous August 15, 1971, decision taking the US and ultimately the world away from the stability of precious metal. From that day forward, America's currency could no longer be redeemed for gold. Overnight, the gold standard was kaput in favor of bureaucrats printing money. Remember when a handful of change weighted down your pocket? They have confiscated all the more precious metals and now our coins feel and weigh like plastic.

"Nixon likely came to regret the destructive forces that his policies had unleashed. Between 1973 and 1974, the Dow Jones Industrial Average lost 45% of its value."[121] While the Dow tanked the Arabs took advantage of the chaos and raised their prices in excess of 70%. The world economic system was unstable because there was no longer a stable common base. Without a gold standard exchange rates become a tool for the bureaucrats to tinker with. Nixon and politicians forward believed they are better equipped to create a fairer economy than the hands off policy of our Founders' laissez-faire.

Floating exchange rates allowed the United States to gradually weaken the dollar under the George W. Bush and Obama administrations in the name of boosting exports and stimulating the economy. Those policies, in turn, fueled the catastrophic real estate and commodity bubbles-and eventual busts-that resulted in the debilitating drop in people's real incomes over the last decade.[122]

"Ever since, the value of the dollar and the rest of the world's currencies have been at the mercy of the U.S. Federal Reserve (the Fed) and other central banks, whose policies reflect the political whims of governments."[123] The fallout and instability of a dollar no longer tied to the gold standard has dramatically hurt our standard of living. "Since 1971 the dollar's purchasing power has declined by more than 80%: since the year 2000, according to the consumer price index (CPI) the dollar's value has declined by about 26%."[124] Nothing has proven positive as the Fed makes one policy blunder after another. When America started printing money, most of the governments around the world followed our lead. The weakened dollar created inflation and uncertainty. Without a stable common standard to trade from such as gold, the world's economy is like a ship adrift at sea without a rudder.

A gold-based measure of money can play the role in economics that the Constitution should play in law. A gold link allows conversion between currencies around the globe; the absence of a gold link invites flights from fiat money and sovereign debt around the globe. Gold forestalls the volatility and high-entropy gyrations that spring from fears of government manipulation and banking fraud. It thus can extend the horizons of the world economy.[125]

"A gold-based measure of money can play the role in economics that the Constitution should play in law," quoted from above, is stunning as America, under the Progressive influence, is operating outside the Constitution and without a guaranteed currency. It's like a person without legs trying to walk - forget keeping up with others.

The latest disaster termed Qualitative Easing (QE) will wreak havoc on future generations to come. Qualitative Easing is yet another form of growing the government. QE is:

> ... focused on buying long-term Treasuries and mortgage-backed securities. This meant that instead of going to the entrepreneurial job creators, loans went primarily to large corporations and to the government itself. It was a form of credit allocation.[126]

Little wonder the federal debt has far more than doubled since 2008 when the Fed kicked off QE. No wonder the unemployment rate is sky high as more and more of our once proud hard working middle class men and women simply give up job hunting and fall through the cracks. How depressing for those out of work who sit idle wondering what is going on. QE has destroyed lives and businesses and will continue to erode our country's productivity unless or until we stop printing money or declare bankruptcy!

The greatest periods of job creation have always been when man is innovating to meet the needs of those around him. Innovations such as autos, PCs, phones, appliances and the Web, to name a few. Henry Ford built cars and at the same time launched a myriad of jobs from auto repair shops to restaurants. Automobiles made viable suburbs and all that goes with them. Innovative entrepreneurs create companies that breed exponential job growth. It's been that way since day one in America. A few more outstanding quotes from Steve Forbes book:

> Cheapening the value of money is not the way to create real sustainable employment. Jobs are created in a healthy economy when entrepreneurs start companies like Starbucks or Staples that succeed in the marketplace. They get capital to expand and hire more people.[127]

> Former congressman Ron Paul sums it up: "If governments or central banks really can create wealth simply by creating money, why does poverty exist anywhere on earth?[128]

QE worked against the recovery because it cut loans to the little guy whose costs are increasing. That same little guy that creates most of the jobs in this once-great country of ours now has no place to go for working capital. By the way, inflation is a form of taxation. Think about it. We are paying mightily and will continue to for government bailouts and increased social programs. It's all bureaucratic sleight of hand. To add further to this bureaucratic sleight of hand, I find it sad and shady that Washington, D.C. cooks the books. Many folks, who after years of sending out resumes and going on job interviews often give up looking for work only to find themselves no longer considered unemployed when the weekly job statistics are announced. Distorted statistics serve no one in the long term as ultimately they often create crashes and bubbles. The only things we know for sure are our debt is soaring skyward second by second as the clock ticks and that inflation is on the horizon.

Once again I fail to understand why constituents continue to reelect such poor leaders. Everyone I talk to knows we are in deep trouble and fears for their childrens' future. We are acting like a bunch of zombies repeatedly buying into Hope and Change. "It is no coincidence that the federal debt has doubled since 2008, the same year that the Fed started implementing QE."[129] People know in their gut we are printing and spending our way into a default. All we have to show for the billions of dollars we have printed and borrowed against is little hope, pocket change and mounting debt.

Nancy Pelosi and President Obama have critiqued Capitalism recently in that it keeps individuals from pursuing their dreams or passions. There is a lack of full time jobs being created for reasons discussed earlier while there remain many part time jobs available in the service industry. Both President Obama and ex-Speaker Pelosi are trying to turn lemons into lemonade by touting part time jobs in that workers will have time to live up to their "full human personality." They will have time to write poetry or whatever they dream while nanny.gov provides them with food stamps, low income housing, free phones and internet not to mention discounted medical care. They have no idea where the money is coming from. If one mentions that this "stuff" is not free because someone had to work to pay for it, then they are quickly labeled mean-spirited, greedy or a bigot.

"A 2013 Rasmussen poll found that an astonishing 74 percent of American adults are in favor of auditing the Federal Reserve and a substantial number think the chairman of the Fed has too much power."[130] Does hauling out a printing press in times of need make any sense at all? There is nothing but faith in the federal reserve system that gives the currency you carry in your wallet or purse any value whatsoever. America is fragile. Pray for Her. Help her by voting for candidates that understand the importance of balancing the budget and working to eliminate our debt.

5

THE PROGRESSIVE AGENDA

"Socialism in all forms-from Wall Street subsidy-seekers to bureaucratic profiteers-
is in practice a conspiracy of the greedy to exploit the productive."
George Gilder

The Progressive movement has a language it of its own. Often, it makes its point by redefining a word.

Our parents taught us that greed meant we were stingy and unwilling to share. Greed was a bad thing and made you a bad person. My little brother and I quickly learned the joy of sharing with one another. The Progressives' definition of greed is; "I don't want to pay more taxes." Men and women paying over 50% of their income in taxes are labeled greedy by the leaders of our country. Imagine giving away 50% or more of what you earn and being viewed as greedy by our country's leaders.

I was taught that compassion was caring for or tending to someone in their time of need. It means a hospital visitation or a note to someone who is down. Compassion is visiting the house bound, donating to the local food shelter or assisting a widow, etc. Compassion has been redefined by the Progressives to mean that the government is going to take more money from taxpayers so they can compassionately spread it around. Big government wants to do the compassioning for us. I don't know about you, but I am compassioned out by the government.

One of the reasons I like Forbes so much is his flat tax proposals. I believe a proportional tax is truly a "fair share" way to deal with taxation plus, as a fantastic by-product, it would minimize the role of the IRS.

> Indeed, the only truly just form of taxation is proportional taxation. Proportional taxation means that everyone who is eligible to pay income taxes pays the same rate. Of course the rich pay more, but they pay proportionally more. So above a certain floor, everyone pays a 10 or 15 or 25 percent federal income tax. Not only is proportional taxation consistent with the constitutional purpose of government-to promote the general, and not particular, welfare - but it also establishes a rule of fairness. It doesn't matter what level of taxation democratic majorities choose, through their elected representatives, as long as the level is imposed on everyone. The current system is a progressive delight because it encourages envy and promotes state-sponsored theft.[131]

If you have any savings you must have an uneasy feeling in your stomach as to where to place it for safe keeping. Ten years ago I had no such fears. Many of my friends are more concerned with holding on to what little they have than risking their nest egg in the stock market, CD's, money markets, precious metals, government bonds, real estate, mutual funds, annuities, etc. Nothing seems safe anymore. How sad and stressful is that. Retirement at age 65. Maybe not.

> Forbes.com contributor Richard Finger puts it bluntly. The Fed's low-interest-rate, easy money policies, he says, "punish the virtuous, the millions of responsible savers....They can no longer count on decent risk-free returns for retirement.[132]

Everything seems unstable, and is, now that our dollars are backed by faith in the federal government and not by gold.

Let me give you some insight into the Progressive mind set. Mike Lux writes for the Huffington Post and is a Progressive's Progressive. He seems shocked that President Obama has really turned America upside down.

Though the recent economic recovery bill was too small and had its flaws, it was literally the biggest single investment in progressive social capital - health care, public education, green jobs, infrastructure, universal broadband - in history. His budget might well be the most audacious and sweeping in progressive history as well - certainly one that competes with LBJ's 1965 budget and FDR's 1935 budget. Obama is fulfilling his promise to the American people in the 2008 campaign: big, bold, truly transformative change.[133]

Mike has that right. Indeed we are living through "big, bold, truly transformative change." Right again. Indeed President Obama did indeed rise to the Progressive challenge instilled in him by his parents and reinforced at Columbia and Harvard Law. Working as a Community Organizer, a la Alinsky, and hobnobbing with Ayers sealed the deal and America's fate. The Huffington Post applauds Obama's track record:

... he is rising to the challenge. And it is imperative that those of us in the progressive movement rise with him. We shouldn't hesitate to say where we disagree, especially on the big things like Iraq, Afghanistan and the banking crisis. And we shouldn't hesitate to push for the best possible policy details - to make sure that health care reform really is universal and has a public plan option for people being screwed by insurance companies, that the climate change policy really is effective and tough in reducing carbon emissions ASAP, and that the budget maximizes investment in the things that matter.

But we should be very clear: Obama has decided to cast his lot with those of us who have been fighting for big, transformative change. If he succeeds, we succeed, and if he fails, we fail - and we fail for at least another generation, because no Democrat will take big risks again for a very long time if Obama loses this gamble.[134]

Notice Progressives concern themselves with "investments in the things that matter" to them (satisfy their agenda) and not the market place. Politicians have wrenched control of the marketplace from innovators, small business owners and folks like you and me. While Hip Hip Hooray is the rally cry for the Progressives the middle class is awash in a myriad of stifling stressful feelings. Out of necessity, their main concern is feeding their family and keeping a roof over their heads. They HOPE things will change back to the way they were "back in the day" so their kids will have the same chances to prosper as they did.

Not everyone is hopeful. "The American Dream is impossible to achieve in this country. So say nearly 6 in 10 people who responded to CNN Money's American Dream Poll, conducted by ORC International. They feel the dream -- however they define it -- is out of reach."[135]

When those concerned with balancing the budget propose tax cuts they are cut off at the knees by Progressives. One would logically think Progressives must consider President Bill Clinton financially irresponsible because he cut taxes masterfully. Clinton's tax cutting legislation is a bit of a tangled web. In 1994, Speaker of the House of Representatives, Newt Gingrich designed and campaigned to implement a "Contract with America." This brought into power a new Republican Congress. President Bill Clinton, being a pragmatist, coalesced and adopted many of the positions of the contract platform. Clinton took credit for a balanced budget and for cutting taxes. However, Clinton merely followed the lead of the Republican Congress.

> We saw this in 1977 when the United States cut taxes. Among the highlights, the Clinton administration cut the capital gains tax from 28% to 20%, and barred new Internet taxes. The economy took off, as did the stock market. Demand for the dollar rose. The Fed didn't meet the demand by supplying enough dollars. The gold price fell.[136]

The difference is Progressives want big government rather than the economy and the stock market to take off. Incredible as it sounds, they believe they should rule the world, i.e. one world, one currency, one god, one border-that being no borders. In other words a Progressive Utopia is a world of United Nations. A United Nations, not a bunch of squabbling little ones like we have today each believing it's sovereignly. One man's dream is another man's nightmare certainly rings true in this instance.

I recommend a book by Adam Fergusson titled, *When Money Dies; The Nightmare of Deficit Spending, Devaluation, and Hyperinflation in Weimar Germany.* The book is a historical account of what happens when a government runs amuck by overspending and overprinting. Comparing the printing of money in 1923 Germany and today Fergusson writes:

...'quantitative easing ', that modern euphemism for surreptitious deficit financing in an electronic era, can no less become an assault on monetary discipline. Whatever the reason for a countries deficit – necessary or profligacy, unwillingness to tax or blindness to expenditure – it is beguiling to suppose that if the day of reckoning is postponed economic recovery will come in time to prevent higher unemployment or deeper recession.[137]

What happens when people no longer have faith in their currency and there is no gold standard? Remember the comic book analogy?

Peoples trust in their currency is here a central theme. As it evaporates, they spend faster, the velocity of circulation increases, a little money does the work of much, prices take off, and more money is needed. The quantity theory of money found its finest object lesson in Germany after the First World War.[138]

The folks in Germany never understood what was happening to them as their life savings dwindled away. They started off trusting their government. The government, as a result of spending more that it took in by taxation, raised and instituted new taxes. They raised taxes to the point that everything came to a grinding gridlock halt. Germans were taxed so harshly and creatively it left them without any pay to take home. Many dropped out of the workforce rather than work for nothing. Human nature kicked in and each class began to believe that taxation should fall on someone else. When the government realized the raising of taxes brought in less revenue, they increased the printing of currency which further increased inflation. Inflation took away any incentive to save. Not surprising, it increased the incentive to spend as spending power was eroding so fast the price of bread was increasing by the hour. The more marks Germany printed, the greater the inflation. Germany was on a treadmill driven by every increasing reams of printed money.

The middle class no longer had enough money to buy the basics and there was nothing left to sell or liquidate. Hyperinflation creates a concern for public order as people no longer have the money to buy a loaf of bread.

The self-confidence of the country ebbed away along with its prosperity, and as it did so the moral degeneration of the nation and its institutions set in. Pessimism and restlessness grew as sense of security, community spirit and patriotism dwindled.[139]

The German people never understood that the printing of money caused their currency's depreciation. Uncertainty ruled everywhere. Nothing seemed to work – their world seemed upside down. As the amount of currency increased in bulk, it decreased in value. Germany could not figure it out but others did before them.

> The more notes were printed, the lower the value fell – illustrating the Copernican thesis expounded by King Sigismund of Poland in 1526 that "money loses its value when it has become too much multiplied."[140]

In 1922 the union leaders "began to demand that wages be fixed on a gold basis."[141] Stability was the name of the game, but no one considered the printing press the root cause of the hyperinflation. "…there is no doubt that party politics continued to rend the country in two when unity was the crying need."[142] Why Germany then and America now does not heed the past is beyond me.

Currency became so devalued it had no serious measure of value and became near worthless as a medium of exchange. As a matter of fact, 1926 became known as the year of the "wheelbarrow" because it took a wheelbarrow full of currency to buy bread. That's a fact. "Whole denominations of mark notes were worthless almost on leaving the press."[143] People shopped with baskets full of banknotes for bread. There was a 100 million mark note printed. People were stressed to the nth. You can imagine how dangerous life became. Everyone did what they had to do to stay alive. They hoarded, they stole and worse. Nothing mattered but staying alive. They were indifferent to everything but food and coal.

There is a very valuable lesson to be learned-"Inflation is the ally of political extremism, the antithesis of order."[144] Incredibly, Germany printed a 100-billiard note (100,000,000,000,000.) One hundred billion. Germany needed to stop all unnecessary spending, tie its currency to something stable and stop the printing presses.

> In 1923, before November, the only increase in animals slaughtered for food had occurred in dogs: after stabilization, the consumption of

every article of daily need – beer, pork, coffee, sugar, tobacco – increased regularly, except dogmeat.[145]

Imagine eating the family pet! Inflation is a terrible thing. It erodes away at the core.

> It remains the case that those who lived with, or who observed, the inflationary process and the crisis of the recovery readily attributed what they saw first and foremost to the inflation; the fear, the greed, the immorality, the demoralization, the dishonest.[146]

> In hyperinflation a kilo of potatoes was worth, to some, more than the family silver; a side of pork more than a grand piano. A prostitute in the family was better than an infant corpse; theft was preferable to starvation; warmth was finer than honor, clothing more essential than democracy, food more needed than freedom.[147]

When it comes to printing money, it seems logical that the longer the mandate to delay "the more savage the cure."[148] I found it fascinating that much of the printing of money was due to war debt. Most of the countries owed war reparations were willing to work with Germany, but the French made life miserable for all concerned as they demanded payment exceeding Germany's ability to pay. Fergusson points out "…the seeds of battle are planted in peace treaties."[149] Inflation made Hitler possible. I encourage you to read Fergusson's book as he details the agony Germany went through and how the Hitlers of this world use chaos to seize control.

I agree with Smith, Forbes and countless others that government serves us best when it stays out of the marketplace.

> Should the Federal Reserve really be in the business of fine-tuning the economy? The Fed was conceived during an agricultural era, when banks making crop loans could face seasonal cash squeezes during harvest time. It was supposed to provide a source of liquidity and also… be a lender of last resort. That is a very different role form the one that it has today: attempting to modulate normal business cycles.

> Equilibrium is the pipe dream of academicians. In real life, the economy is not an engine, but a dynamic, serendipitous stew of human

actions, needs and desires. Unpredictable events constantly arise to thwart the earnest intentions of bureaucrats. The Fed-indeed, any government bureaucracy-is no more capable of successfully orchestrating the economic activities of millions of people that it would be to control the weather.[150]

The fed's grip on our money supply did not begin with QE. The fed over stirred the pot under President George W. Bush in massaging interest rates. Economists actually caused the financial crisis.

To appreciate the depth of the political upheaval created by the 2008 financial crisis, just tally the power shifts that occurred in its wake. In addition to the turmoil in the Middle East, 13 out of 17 European governments changed over as a result of the initial financial crisis. In the United States, the stock market panic in September 2008 reversed the slight lead of John McCain and helped sweep the far-left Barak Obama into office.[151]

Forbes makes the point that there is profit in chaos for someone. America wanted change and unfortunately got it.

Forbes raises an issue which points to the Progressive agenda: "The media blamed this breakdown of social trust on Wall Street greed. They should have blamed the Fed."[152] If you listened to the main stream media or read the liberal daily newspaper, you would come to the conclusion that the massive foreclosures were due to large greedy banks or large gluttonous corporations (mortgage institutions). America, we are shooting ourselves in the foot. If you get down to brass tacks Occupy Wall Street should have been Occupy Fed.

It's not just government and banks that stiff citizens and walk away from their loans. The destruction of money corrupts social trust and morality among ordinary citizens as well. In 2011, in the wake of the financial crisis, the *New York Times* ran an astonishing story, "They Walked Away and They're Glad They Did," a sympathetic look at people who had decided to abandon their mortgages in the wake of the financial crisis.[153]

Many homeowners felt it was their right to simply push the reset button and walk away from their mortgage commitments. Progressives believe in relative truth so therefore there is no real debt if it no longer works for you. Hard to get your head around isn't it? "The *Times* quoted a Harvard University housing expert who backed them up": "If your home is a financial asset, and it's financially rational to walk away, that's what you do." That's what you do?! Isn't it astounding and self-defeating that our government is picking up much of the tab through various mechanisms which ultimately trickles down to the honest taxpayer.

> The mortgage defaults that came anyway and triggered the collapse came not from the aggregate inability of debtors to pay as the economists calculated, but from the free acts of homebuyers. Having bet on constantly rising home prices, they simple folded their hands and walked away when the value of their houses collapsed. The bankers had accounted for everything but free will.[154]

A good illustration of a city literally imploding due to massive debt is the City of Detroit, Michigan, and the many abandoned houses, churches, factories and other buildings now being vandalized and wasting away due to neglect.

There was far more impacting the foreclosure market than new homeowners walking away from recently purchased homes whose market value dropped when the bubble burst. There were also the numerous homeowners who used their homes as an ATM to finance new cars, televisions, vacations, etc. Had they not used their home as a line of credit, they might have weathered the storm. Economics 101 wisely teaches that you only borrow against your home for medical expenses or college tuition. America was once a country of savers and that sense of thrift made for stability. History has proven over and over again that countries whose citizens save are stronger because of it. Today we want what we want NOW. Why should we have concern about the longer term ramifications? We, American's best, prepare ourselves for a major downward adjustment, by preparing to adjust to a change, in our standard of living.

Many rich are eating from the Nanny State pie. I believe the last election asked and answered the following question by David B. Muhlhausen and Patrick D. Tyrrell of the Heritage Foundation.

> Americans have reached a point in the life of their republic at which the democratic political process has become a means for many voters

to defend and expand the "benefits" they receive from government. Do Americans want a republic that encourages and validates a growing dependence on the state and a withering of civil society?

People by nature will take the easy way when presented with a fork in the road. I have a retired school teacher friend who brags about casting her vote in favor of her "pocketbook." She is living a comfortable middle class retirement but votes for the candidate that will give her the most "freebies." Nothing else matters. If something is free, then little concern, if any, is given the taxpayer plodding along at the other side of the so called free transaction. The Progressives have a game plan that, in my opinion, is going to bring down this great country of ours unless we get a grip on things. We must unleash our brightest and most innovative by granting them loans and eliminating the regulatory grip. When one cuts to the chase, innovation is the source of profit. The quickest and most efficient way to fix our economy is to let innovators innovate.

I recently read a book by George Gilder, titled *Knowledge and Power: The Information Theory of Capitalism and How it is Revolutionizing our World,* which I found to be incredibly enlightening:

> Entrepreneurship is devoted to creation of goods and services. Creativity is always surprising. That is why it cannot be planned or demanded by governments or even by customers. As Steve Jobs put it, explaining his contempt for market surveys, "It's really hard to design products by focus groups. A lot of times people don't know what they want until you show it to them." As Henry Ford said many years earlier: "If I had listened to my customers, I would have built a faster horse."[155]

Gilder points out that between 1996 and 2009 neatly all new jobs were the result of startups. Even in the midst of the depression (2009), new companies added 2.3 million jobs. Let's take a look at the type of jobs the Progressive agenda brings to the table and their impact. ObamaCare –

> It provides for 16,000 new IRS agents and new taxes and fees galore to fund it, but it actually degrades the power of physicians and restricts the supply of medical instruments with new taxes and regulations. The gap between knowledge and power is filled with government rules and price controls.[156]

There is nothing efficient when Washington, D.C. escalates the role of government and degrades the role of the individual worker be he a doctor or a butcher. Gilder points out:

> For all the billions of dollars wasted on Solyndras and windmills, a few score million were invested in natural gas fracking experiments that yielded trillions of new cubic feet and hundreds of billions of dollars' worth of new asset value from Pennsylvania to North Dakota.[157]

Pipelines which would bring jobs of all sorts to America are delayed to favor many crony capitalist boondoggles with nothing left to show for the investment but billions of taxpayer dollars down the tubes.

Speaking of debt creation, ObamaCare may take the cake as its ramifications are exponential. Health care could be viewed as an opportunity if managed carefully but alas:

> The opportunity is obscured by government bureaucracy, price controls, and regulatory glut. With its 16,000 new IRS agents and no new doctors, Obamacare also restricts new medical instruments with a 3.2-percent tax on gross receipts that can capture more than 100 percent of profits. The Food and Drug Administration's rules are particularly hostile to health care innovation, adding a billion-dollar toll over seven years to the launch of a new pharmaceutical. This federal structure pushes drug companies to focus on sex and lifestyle pills with huge markets rather than on new drugs that can keep people alive and working.[158]

> In the perverse feedback loops of free goods, free health care comes to mean hypochondria and needless illness caused by needless exams and treatments, queues for an ever expanding political portfolio of mediocre services, and-at the end of the line-euthanasia under government bureaucracy. Free drugs lead to widespread drug addiction to existing medications and an end to medical innovation. Free money, manifested in the zero-interest-rate policy of the Federal Reserve, divert the wealth of savers to favored governments and crony capitalists while creating shortages for everyone else.[159]

I am sick of all the political rhetoric about spreading the wealth. Capitalism serves others naturally. We should be proud of all we do and what we stand for.

The fact that a worker in a Nike factory in Vietnam has a lower quality of life than a worker in the United States "feels wrong to many of us," Romer said in another interview, "but that's not the question here. The question is, did Nike's coming in make the life of that person better off or worse off? The unambiguous answer is that Nike coming in really helps that person and helps many other people in that country.[160]

Truth is not relative but poverty is.

We have made many mistakes recently, but it is not too late. We must learn from our mistakes and act with boldness and confidence NOT with gridlock. Gilder pulls no punches:

The great mistake of the Bush and Obama administrations' response to the crisis of 2008 was to shield the owners from the cost of their mistakes. By guaranteeing things, government tends to destroy their value, which depends on dedicated ownership. In the United States, the Constitution guarantees only the right of property, not to its worth-or so it seemed until recently.[161]

Whatever the inequality of incomes, it is dwarfed by the inequality of contributions to human advancement. As the science fiction writer Robert Heinlein wrote, "Throughout history, poverty is the normal condition of man. Advances that permit this norm to be exceeded-here and there, now and then-are the work of an extremely small minority, frequently despised, often condemned, and almost always opposed by all right-thinking people. Whenever this tiny minority is kept from creating, or (as sometimes happens) is driven out of society, the people slip back into abject poverty. This is known as 'bad luck.'" President Obama unconsciously confirmed Heinlein's sardonic view of human nature in a campaign speech in Iowa: "We had reversed the recession, avoided depression, got the economy moving again, but over the last six months we've had a run of bad luck.[162]

The average small business owner spends more time dealing with government regulations than with his customers. Every new regulation results in a decrease in productivity. Decreased productivity results in decreased revenue.

Lower revenue results in less employees. We keep this up, and the only help wanted ads will be government ones to write more regulations and enforce the ones on the books. Do you think our rivals in Asia are fixating on rules and regulations or increasing output? They build new factories while we produce paperwork in response to one government agency or another.

6

PROGRESSIVE ATTACKS

"The great mistake of the Bush and Obama administrations' response to the
crisis of 2008
was to shield the owners from the cost of their mistakes.
By guaranteeing things, government tends to destroy their value,
which depends on dedicated ownership.
In the United States, the Constitution guarantees only the right of property,
not to its worth-or so it seemed until recently."
George Gilder

Attacks on the Way We Do Business

My mother and most of her friends would be caged in state penitentiaries if they raised children today. The parenting methodology back in the 50s and 60s involved techniques that would be considered obsolete, out of style, or downright dangerous to many of today's government agencies. Our moms sent us out to play unsupervised for hours at a time. We were left to our own devices and soon learned how to entertain ourselves and get along with others. We knew how far from the house we could wander without getting into trouble. We walked to school or to the bus carrying our homework and lunch box. There were no SUVs and vans cued up for blocks at the entrance of the school preparing to drop off or pick up sons or daughters heavily laden with book bags as if time were of the essence. Imagine - walking to and from school was considered a way of life. It must have attributed to our well-being as I recall no talk of childhood obesity. The higher the grade you were in the longer the walk the school district demanded before a bus pick up was assigned. I walked almost one half mile to my elementary school. Life was simple. We walked and talked. There was no fear of broken limbs from tripping while walking and texting simultaneously.

While recently checking out my Facebook stream the following headline caught my eye –

Father Convicted & Punished for Making Son Walk a Mile Home from School.[163]

Robert Demond was sentenced to a one-year probation, a $200 fine and to a child parenting class for a misdemeanor charge of second-degree endangering the welfare of a minor…

Demond told the judge that it was a common form of punishment when he was a kid and that he didn't see it as morally wrong or criminal. He had picked his son up from school and questioned him about a matter that came to his attention. When his son didn't respond, he stopped the vehicle and made him walk home to think about his actions.

"How far did you make him walk?" asked Judge Kathleen Watanabe.

"About a mile," Demond said.[164]

The 5th Circuit Court Judge pontificated that walking home from school, as a form of discipline, is considered "old school" and no longer appropriate. Give me a break. Not only did the poor parent endure a lecture from the judge. He was forced to pay a fine and a sit through a state run parenting class. I wonder how much it costs and how much time it took the government to develop and implement a parenting course. I assume it would include tasks such as funding the project, hiring bureaucrats to develop, write and approve the course, the hiring of administrators to pull it all together, including scheduling the students, hiring and training an instructor and locating a building or room in which to hold classes. Plus, if there are printed handouts required, the printing job would, by law, be put out for bid which requires even more administrators. You gotta love it. All because Ms. Judge truly believes she has the ability to raise someone else's child better than the ones that tended to him from birth.

It seems to me the lesson learned is clear – one need no longer obey his parents as long as the authorities have the final say in our households. The Fifth Circuit Court in Hawaii may come in and act as head of the household should you choose to discipline your child as you see fit. It would not surprise me if today's ruling secularists were to decree that all parents must read the illustrious Hillary Rodham Clinton's book *It Takes a Village*.

When I was growing up, life was good. We were blessed and knew it. Numerous times daily, our mom thanked God for everything He provided. I remember setting up a front yard lemonade stand in Royal Oak, Michigan. I dragged out a card table and made a sign out of construction paper and crayons while mom made the lemonade. The neighbors obliged by buying a paper cup full of my lemonade for five cents a glass. I received many "atta girls" that day and also learned what a tip was. More importantly, I learned a little about setting up a business.

> In Midway, Georgia, a 14-year-old girl and her 10 year old sister sold lemonade from their front yard. Two police officers bought some. But the next day, different officers ordered them to close their stand.
>
> Their father went to city hall to try to find out why. The clerk laughed, and said she didn't know. Eventually, Police Chief Kelly Morningstar explained, "We were not aware of how the lemonade was made, who made the lemonade, and of what the lemonade was made with."[165]

I ended up an executive with Pan American Airways and a successful Century 21 Real Estate office owner thanks, in no little part, to life experiences such as the organizing and selling I did as a child. I fear, that the poor girls from Midway, Georgia, may well end up working for the government creating ever more rules and regulations due to their life lessons.

All the girls in my class sold Girl Scout cookies. I worked hard to sell the most in my troop, but fell short. I missed a mark I set for myself, but I learned I needed to work harder and smarter the following year. Officials in Hazelwood,

Missouri ordered little girls to <u>stop selling Girl Scout Cookies</u>.[166] The city sent the Mills family a letter saying that selling cookies in front of their home without a permit violated the city's home occupancy codes.[167]

I learned a very positive lesson selling Girl Scout Cookies while the Girl Scouts in Hazelwood learned that the government controls many facets of their lives including fund-raising on their front yard. I presume from their actions, that the officials in Hazelwood prefer young Girl Scouts to knock on the front doors of strangers then peddle their boxes of cookies on their front lawn in sight and earshot of mom.

John Stossel decided to open a lemon aid stand in New York City. Below he comments on what NYC expects of prospective lemonade vendors:

1) Register as sole proprietor with the County Clerk's Office (must be done in person)

2) Apply to the IRS for an Employer Identification Number.

3) Complete 15-hr Food Protection Course!

4) After the course, register for an exam that takes 1 hr. You must score 70% to pass. (Sample question: "What toxins are associated with the puffer fish?") If you pass, allow 3-5 weeks for delivery of Food Protection Certificate.

5) Register for sales tax Certificate of Authority

6) Apply for a Temporary Food Service Establishment Permit. Must bring copies of the previous documents and completed forms to the Consumer Affairs Licensing Center.

Then, at least 21 days before opening your establishment, you must:

Arrange for an inspection with the Health Department's Bureau of Food Safety and Community Sanitation. It takes about 3 weeks to get your appointment. If you pass, you can set up a business once you:

Buy a portable fire extinguisher from a company certified by the FDNY and set up a contract for waste disposal...

Had we been able to schedule our health inspection and open my stand legally, it would have taken us 65 days.[168]

Stossel went ahead and sold lemonade without obtaining New York City's approval. He claimed he looked "dumb" selling his lemonade with a big fire extinguisher taking up space on the table. Obviously, we are having fun, at New York City's expense, but maybe, just maybe a child with a card table selling lemonade on his/her front stoop does not require government oversight. Where is the common sense?

Politicians say, "We support entrepreneurs," but the bureaucrats make it hard. The Feds alone add 80,000 pages of new rules every year. Local governments add more. There are so many incomprehensible rules that even the bureaucrats can't tell you what's legal. In the name of public safety, politicians strangle opportunity.[169]

Today's ruling Progressives believe a neighbor's front yard lemonade stand is in need of public safety oversight. By the way, my lemonade stand had oversight. Mom's oversight regulations made more sense than the government's. If I dropped a cup on the grass, I was to throw it away. I was taught to use prongs and not touch the ice cubes. I was to keep my hands and the card table clean at all times, and I was to patrol the area for any napkins that might have blown off the table. Mom watched me like a hawk from the living room window. Be honest. Would you prefer a glass of my mom's lemonade or one purchased from a stand somewhere in New York City?

Speaking of parental oversight...

It seems Christy Duffy took her 17-year-old daughter to her local doctor's office for a physical and was stunned to see a sign that read...

ATTENTION PARENTS OF ADOLESCENT CHILDREN AGE 7y-12y.
New Michigan Medical Records access laws have been put in place.
This will require a nurse to have a short 5 minute private conversation with your child.
We will explain the purpose and process at the time of the visit and answer any questions you many have.[170]

The quote below is from Christy Duffy's blog...

I was there last week for an appointment for Amy. She hurt her foot, which makes dancing difficult, so we had to get that checked out. Amy is 17; I asked if this policy was in effect and if so, how could I opt out. The receptionist told me it's a new law and there is no opting out. Working to keep my cool, I said, "I'm sure there is." She said, "No, there isn't." At which point I asked if I needed to leave and go to the urgent care center because I was not submitting my daughter to such a conversation.

That did not go over well.

The receptionist closed the window. Almost immediately, the office manager turned the corner and said, "Mrs. Duffy, may I speak with you?"

She said there was a new policy that would allow a child to access his/her medical records online and the child would be allowed to block a parent from viewing the website. The nurse would also inform my children that the doctor's office is a safe place for them to receive information about STDs, HIV and birth control. That is what the nurse would be chatting about with my children without any pesky parental oversight.

I kindly informed her that no one would be talking with my children privately, and I needed to know how to opt out of this policy before bringing Amy back for her physical next month. (Yay for physicals! Amy is so excited.)

By this time, the doctor was ready to see Amy so I had to cut the conversation short because I was not letting my girl out of my eyesight or earshot. Not when it was clear that these people were angling to undermine my parental authority.

Does that sound a bit dramatic to you? It shouldn't. Because that is exactly what they are trying to do.

Make sure this is crystal clear: what they want to do is talk to your child about sex and drugs (maybe rock and roll – who knows?) without your input. Is it really such a stretch to imagine that a doctor who does not value abstinence before marriage would encourage your daughters – as young as 12! – to receive birth control? Is it really such a stretch to imagine a nurse telling a young boy – because a 12 year old boy is a BOY – that she will give him condoms so he can be "safe"? Is this what you want told to your children without the ability to filter the info through your world view?

Should a doctor ever ask to speak to a child without a parent present? If he/she suspects abuse then of course. But short of evidence of abuse, a doctor should not need to speak to a child alone.

I am the Mom. I will pick who can talk to my kids about sex and drugs. And rock-n-roll for that matter.

Regardless what health care provider you choose, please know that no one has the right to remove you from your child's exam room. Perhaps if more of us stood up for our rights as parents, this ludicrous undermining of parental authority might end.[171]

Good on Mrs. Duffy for not only going eyeball-to-eyeball with her doctor but telling her story nationally. I found Mrs. Duffy's blog originally on my Facebook stream but after doing some research, I found her blog had gone viral which is no easy feat. Have you been to the doctor's lately and been handed multiple pages of questions having little to do with the visit? I have and I chose not to answer them. As far as I know there it is no law, stating you must bare your soul to the doctor's computer which is linked to the ACA. Here are a few example questions from a New York based doctor; (1) Are there guns located in your household? (2) Were you ever in the armed services? If I require antibiotics for a sore throat why should my doctor ask about gun ownership? The federal government's attempts to take the place of parents is downright scary given its track record of ineptness. I know my mom would have pivoted and pulled either Mark or myself out of Mrs. Duffy's Doctor's office. Our mother was an RN, turned stay at home mom who would have felt the doctor was "nuts!"

The youth at Kings Baptist Church in Vero Beach, Florida, every now and then hold a free car wash. I believe it is primarily for seniors (although no one is turned away) who might find it difficult to give their vehicle a great cleaning inside and out. It is simply a way to give back and show their love. Fund raising car washes are pretty all American if you ask me. Forget about charity car washes if you live in Arlington, Virginia:

Teams, clubs and activity groups at Arlington Public Schools have been banned from doing car wash fundraisers because of stormwater regulations.

According to the county's Department of Environmental Services, APS was issued its first stormwater permit by the state last month, after more stringent stormwater regulations were passed by the Virginia General Assembly in July 2013. **The permit disallows all charity car washes on school property.**

Washington-Lee, Yorktown and Wakefield High Schools notified their teams and clubs this week that they were no longer allowed to conduct such fundraisers.

"There is an important underlying reason why most types of car washing are not allowed under state and federal stormwater regulations," said DES spokeswoman Shannon Whalen McDaniel. "The chlorinated water, detergents, petroleum products, and other pollutants that get washed into the storm drain system are carried into our local streams, the Potomac River and ultimately, to the Chesapeake Bay. As a result, there are educational and environmental benefits that come with finding new and environmentally friendly ways to raise money for extracurricular activities.[172]

Needless to say, coaches and students are not happy with the ban. What about moving the fundraising event to private property?

…according to DES Watershed Programs Manager Jason Papacosma. All car washes that aren't for personal use require a specific permit or written determination from the state, even charity car washes held on private property.[173]

Not to worry. The bureaucrats have promised to suggest alternatives to fundraise that are green. Whoopee. I bet if the Arlington schools were to hold a bake sale, the sugar and calorie police, led by our First Lady, would sic yet another agency on our fledging entrepreneurs. Liberal secularist Progressives would have us believe there is no need to raise funds. All that needs to be done is to raise the school taxes to provide funding to meet needs they deem appropriate. Another lesson learned.

I find it fascinating that if you live in socialist Europe (the Progressive's wanna-be prototype government); "You can't wash your own car in your own driveway. That might hurt the environment, so you must take your vehicle to a government-approved car wash and wildly overpay someone else to do it for you."[174] See what we have to look forward to if we keep electing the same lot repeatedly? The hours I spent at charity car washes taught me a thing or two about teamwork and organization. Mom never chastised me for coming home wet and soapy. She would laugh and tell me to take my clothes off in the laundry room before I messed up the house. Life was simple, good, and common sense prevailed.

No matter when I glance at a newspaper, listen to TV or scroll through Facebook, I encounter numerous examples of regulatory overreach. One could write book after book laying out examples. I am offering up a few to prove the point. To obtain more details, merely Bing my footnotes. Let's begin with rainwater:

> You may not be aware of this, but many Western states, including Utah, Washington and Colorado, have long outlawed individuals from collecting rainwater on their own properties because, according to the officials, *that rain belongs to someone else.*[175]

Moving on to power plants and climate change, IJR Review wrote earlier this year:

> In his latest and most sweeping effort to combat "climate change" (aka, "global warming," "climate disruption," "the end of the world as we know it"), President Barack Obama has directed the Environmental Protection Agency to issue new rules on carbon emissions by America's power plants.
>
> It's not like he didn't tell us from the beginning *exactly* what he planned to do. For those in need of a refresher, here's Obama in 2009:
>
> **"Under my plan of a cap and trade system, electricity prices will necessarily skyrocket."**
>
> Yeah, cap and trade is back. Despite being soundly rejected by Congress a few years ago. Hey, it's not like Obama has let Congress get in his way in the past, right? (See: DOMA, DREAM Act, Federal Immigration Law)
>
> On Monday, Obama's EPA will unveil a new rule limiting the amount of carbon emissions from America's coal power plants:
>
> *The rule will impose a cap on the level of emissions existing power plants are permitted and it will provide each state a series of options to implement the cap.*

Among other options, power plants will be allowed to increase the energy they derive from renewable sources like <u>wind and solar power</u>, adopt new technology to increase energy efficiency, and join or create a <u>statewide cap-and-trade system</u> to effectively tax the excess carbon emissions.

Obama explained the unilateral action on Saturday:

"Today, about 40 percent of America's carbon pollution comes from power plants. But right now, there are no national limits to the amount of carbon pollution that existing plants can pump into the air we breathe — none.

That's why, a year ago, I directed the Environmental Protection Agency to...come up with commonsense guidelines for reducing dangerous carbon pollution from our power plants."

While the president claimed that the new "guidelines" were developed in "an open and transparent way, with input from the business community," let's not forget this quote from 2008:

"So if somebody wants to build a coal-powered plant, they can; <u>it's just that it will bankrupt them</u> because they're going to be charged a huge sum for all that <u>greenhouse gas</u> that's being emitted."

Greenhouse gases. It's always about greenhouse gases with the global-warming crowd.

Yet, a 2013 report from Obama's own darling – the United Nations – found that the effect of greenhouse gas on the environment have been vastly overstated. But, to borrow a question from Hillary, when your objective is to bankrupt the coal industry, what difference does it matter?[176]

"Unauthorized Charity"

How about feeding the poor?

Homelessness is hardly an invisible problem in the United States, but some cities wish that it were — and as a result, are moving to ban feeding the homeless.

Thirty-three cities have already implemented these policies according to the National Coalition for the Homeless, and at least four municipalities — Daytona Beach, Florida; Raleigh, N.C.; Myrtle Beach, S.C.; and Birmingham, Alabama — have recently fined, removed, or threatened prison time against individuals and private groups that have fed the homeless.

Director of community organizing for the National Coalition for the Homeless, Michael Stoops, said that he wished cities would stop trying to ban the charitable acts:

"Homeless people are visible in downtown America. And cities think by cutting off the food source it will make the homeless go away. It doesn't, of course," Stoops said, "We want to get cities to quit doing this. We support the right of all people to share food.[177]

The next story to me is heart wrenching and undercuts acts of kindness favor of the "Nanny State." The headline alone should make the hair stand up on the back of your neck.

Town bans acts of charity because it undercuts need for government agencies.

DAYTONA BEACH, FL — A charitable couple that devotes weekly time to feeding the homeless and hungry have been slapped with matching $375 fines as recognition for their acts of kindness. The town and county are deploying police to forcefully stop and punish people who privately feed the homeless because it reduces the need for government-run social services.

The couple behind the project is Chico and Debbie Jimenez, a middle-aged Christian couple that has devoted their time to feed the downtrodden every Wednesday in Manatee Island Park in Daytona Beach. Debbie, 52, is a retired auto parts store manager, and Chico, 60, is a retired construction manager. The couple both left their jobs a year ago to devote themselves fully to their ministry, called Spreading the Word Without Saying a Word.

The Jimenez's use the Book of Matthew as inspiration during their extensive feeding efforts. As Jesus said:

"For I was hungry and you gave me something to eat, I was thirsty and you gave me something to drink, I was a stranger and you invited me in, I needed clothes and you clothed me, I was sick and you looked after me, I was in prison and you came to visit me…. Truly I tell you, whatever you did for one of the least of these brothers and sisters of mine, you did for me." (Matthew 35:34-40)

After a year of service, their efforts were abruptly squashed by the government in May 2014, when 5 police officers were sent to shut down their ministry. The officers "made no bones about it," according to the Jimenez's; everyone responsible for feeding the homeless would be punished to the full extent of the law.

Chico and Debbie Jimenez, along with four volunteers, were each given 2nd Degree Misdemeanors. The penalty for unauthorized charity is a $375 fine imposed on every volunteer. One of the volunteers was a wheelchair-bound man who had recently escaped homelessness. As an additional slap in the face, police handed out multiple parking tickets to the organizers. In total, police dumped $2,238.00 in fines on the peaceful volunteers.

Additionally, all members involved were permanently banned from the park. If any should return, they will be arrested for trespassing — on public property, no less. The right to peaceably assemble has been declared null-and-void for charity workers.

"You've got to have permits," the officers insisted.

"The worst thing is, these are people we have grown to love, they've become like family to us, and now we're not allowed to go down and do that anymore. It's just heartbreaking. I have cried and cried and cried," said Debbie Jimenez.[178]

The quote "penalty for unauthorized charity" is for real. Now, THIS is a real example of "mean spirited." Our Founders, Roger and I believe that most Americans would advocate rewards for charity, not fines. How pathetic have we become when we keep reelecting the same "nuts" into office?

Moving on to gun control:

Arizona Student Suspended For Having Gun Screen Saver

A student in Florence, Arizona was suspended last week because he had a picture of a gun on his computer. The incident is yet another in a long line of ridiculous knee jerk reactions by schools all over the nation in response to the December Sandy Hook shooting.

A local ABC affiliate reported that Daniel McClaine Jr., a freshman at Poston Butte High School, was turned in to school officials by a teacher who noticed he had saved a picture of an AK-47 as his desktop background on his school lap top.

The school suspended McClaine, citing district policy which states that students are barred from "sending or displaying offensive messages or pictures," and should refrain from creating, accessing and/or distributing pictures that may be considered "harassing, threatening, or illegal."

The School District, released the following statement:

Although we cannot specifically discuss student discipline, we can certainly agree that violence in schools is a sensitive and timely issue. Students, parents and staff are on edge, and the daily news delivers more reasons for caution. All of us must work together to protect our kids and to cultivate an environment that is conducive to learning.

McClaine contested his suspension, saying that the image is not threatening.

"This gun wallpaper does not show anything that's violent. It's not showing anybody getting shot in any way. It's just a picture of a gun. It's nothing — nobody getting shot, nobody getting it pointed at them, it's nothing," the student told reporters.

After reporters got hold of the story, the school backed down and allowed McClaine to return to classes earlier than originally planned.

McClaine's father stated "To me it's ridiculous. Three days for a picture? It wasn't like he was standing in front of the school holding the gun. He should have got a warning. He shouldn't have ever been suspended. Not for something so frivolous."

This case is far from isolated, as we have seen over the past days and weeks, in the wake of the Sandy Hook shooting. It is now a daily occurrence.[179]

This one is a classic which I titled **"Pop Tart Pistol."**

An attorney for the family of an Anne Arundel County second-grader suspended from school for nibbling a pastry into the shape of a gun said Monday that a top school official has denied the appeal to have the boy's record expunged.

Robin Ficker, attorney for Park Elementary School student Josh Welch and his family, said he will now appeal to the county school board.

Josh Welch was suspended in March for two days after school officials accused him of shaping the pastry into the form of a gun and waving it around.

Last month, Ficker said he met with school officials in an attempt to have the suspension expunged, but no resolution was reached.

That sent the matter to Superintendent Kevin Maxwell. Ficker said Monday that he received a letter from a school official acting as the superintendent's designee who said the appeal request was denied.

Anne Arundel County schools spokesman Bob Mosier declined to comment on the matter.

Ficker said he has 30 days to appeal to the county school board and will likely do so this week.

"I've spoken to Mr. Welch, and we're definitely going to appeal to the board of education," said Ficker, referring to Josh's father, J.B. Welch. "If this school can't educate a 7-year-old without putting him out of school, how are they going to deal with 17-year-olds?[180]

This one is more "stupider" as our President would say. I call it **"Bubble Trouble."**

A Pennsylvania elementary school allegedly suspended a 5-year-old girl for making a "terrorist threat" after the child told a friend that she was going to shoot her with a pink Hello Kitty bubble gun.

The unidentified kindergartener was initially suspended for 10 days following the Jan. 10 incident at Mount Carmel Area Elementary School in Northumberland County, PennLive.com reported.

"This little girl is the least terroristic person in Pennsylvania," Robin Ficker, a lawyer for the girl's family, told the website.

Ficker said that the girl did not have the toy gun, which blows soapy bubbles, on her at school when she suggested that she and a friend shoot each other.[181]

Good grief! The soapy plump little pink transparent gun has a kitty on the handle and would scare no one but a bureaucrat. The only play gun less scary or realistic might be one made of Legos. The headline reads:

Massachusetts boy, 5, warned by school for making Lego toy gun

A 5-year-old boy in Massachusetts may be suspended after he reportedly built a toy gun out of Legos during an after-school program.

Joseph Cardosa, the student, is part of the after-school program at Hyannis West Elementary School, on Cape Cod, MyFoxBoston.com reported.

A few days ago, his parents received a letter that said the boy has received his first written warning for using toys inappropriately, and that upon a second written warning, he will be suspended from the program for two weeks.

The boy's parents, Shelia Cruz and Octavio Cardosa, say the school is taking things too far.[182]

When pregnant with their first child, my sister-in-law Laura, and my brother Mark, requested that I never purchase my nephew Ryan any toy guns. I thought this was a tad too protective, but of course I honored her request without comment. A few years later, while visiting in Texas, I noticed toy guns in the house. When asked about it Laura replied, "Oh Sue! I gave up. Little boys turn everything into a toy gun."

Moving on. What would be less intimidating than a Pink Kitty soapy bubble gun or a Lego gun? If I were writing fiction, I would be unable to make this stuff up. The headline reads:

Students Suspended for Nerf Guns at School.

Several school kids from Washington were recently suspended for having Nerf guns at school.

Not surprising considering the Edmonds School District has a "zero tolerance" policy on guns, but the fact that a teacher said it was okay, has parents perturbed.

The incident happened last Friday before class at Chase Lake Elementary School when a sixth grade boy brought a number of the soft foam projectile guns to class as part of a project – which was allegedly approved by a teacher. So, as boys are known to do, they played around with the toys before class.

"So he took them out and of course — Nerf gun — they started testing how far they would shoot," said parent Shannon Shumard.

Although Shumard's son and daughter didn't bring the Nerf guns to school, they both participated playing with them and were suspended for a day. The suspension means her kids won't be able to take high school algebra or serve on the student council.

"They are both very upset," Shumard said. "I mean, it's a day suspension, but it's a permanent on their record."

Stacey Leidholm's son, who she said has straight As, received the same punishment.

"I do understand that they definitely need consequences, but not that harsh of a consequence," she said.

The school district confirms the incident occurred, but refuses to divulge particulars. According to school district spokeswoman Amanda Ralston: "Again, it's a matter of safety and it's of the utmost importance. So even if it's a toy, we take it seriously,"

But parents believe the district overreacted, particularly because a teacher gave the kids permission.

"If the teacher and the school staff don't even know their own rules, how are the children supposed to know them?" Shumard said.[183]

Imagine a teacher asking little boys and girls to bring toy guns to school then suspending them for playing with them. Considering the way political correctness is catching on in America. I, too, like the parents in the article, would be concerned with "having Nerf guns at school" being on my kids permanent record. Maybe, just maybe, one day down the road, one of these children might lose a job to a child that did not play with guns. It would not surprise me if some "Human Resource" type were to find a child that played with guns not suitable for employment. Personally I think the teacher is a coward.

Here is another classic:

Where would the Founding Fathers stand on a right to bear pencils?

A second-grader was suspended from school for two days for pretending his pencil was a gun while playing with his friend in class Friday.

"It's an effort to try to get kids not to bring any form of violence into the classroom, even if it's violent play," school spokesperson Bethanne Bradshaw said.

During a game of make-believe, Christopher Marshall, 7, imagined he was a Marine like his father Paul Marshall, who thinks his kid was just being a typical boy. He and his wife Wendy Marshall said the Driver Elementary School in Suffolk, Va. is overreacting.

"I find it ridiculous that he cannot use his imagination and be a boy," Wendy Marshall told the Daily News. "When my son wants to pretend he's a Marine or a Navy pilot like his granddad or an auto mechanic like his other granddad, I don't think that should be an issue."

Bradshaw said that the school has a zero-tolerance policy for weapons. She thinks that a pencil can be considered a weapon if someone makes gun noises while pointing the weapon at another person in a threatening way.

Christopher said that he is sorry and will not pretend to play with guns in school any more. His parents were quick to point out that, according to the suspension note, Christopher stopped when the teacher told him to do so.

The other student, also 7, was suspended as well.

Paul Marshall understands that people feel uneasy about guns in schools considering the onslaught of recent school shootings but feels that Driver Elementary School failed to use common sense.

"It's gone too far. Enough is enough," he told local station Fox 43. "Where do we draw the line? A pencil - was it sharpened? Was it now? Is it a No. 2? I mean what's the big deal? He's just being a kid.[184]

And last, but not least, as I know you are about gunned out:

Bang! You're suspended: Maryland children punished for making gun gestures

Two 6-year-old boys from Maryland were suspended from their school for making gun gestures during a harmless game of pretend, leaving parents outraged.

Officials at a Talbot County Elementary School disciplined the boys after they were playing a game of cops and robbers according to Baltimore station WJZ-TV. It was the second such incident in the state in recent weeks.

"It's ridiculous." Julia Merchant, mother of one of the children said to the channel.

Last month, 6-year-old Rodney Lynch was suspended from his Montgomery County school for making the same gesture twice.

"Just pointing your fingers like this, and then she did the 'pow' sound, and I just went like that and then I got sent to the office again," the boy told WJZ-TV at the time.

"They're saying he threatened a student, threatened to shoot a student," the boy's father, Rodney Lynch Sr. said after the suspension. "He was playing."

A child psychologist told WJZ-TV that the minds of most 6-year-olds are not developed enough to understand why adults might be sensitive to the gesture.[185]

It's not as though we are operating as a police state. It's more like a stupid state. We will get more into this in the next chapter, but why will your school district gladly, and I mean gladly, hand your 13-year-old free condoms yet suspend him for holding his pencil like a gun?

The over-regulation on the local level falls far short of the shenanigan's in Washington, D.C. It is constant and far more rampant in our nation's capital.

One of the most provocative examples of overreach on the Federal level is the IRS and how it used its clout to ensure the reelection of Barak Obama. The delaying and harassing of non-profits and the release of conservative groups tax information puts the IRS on par with Orwell's Nineteen Eighty-Four, Big Brother. One of the reasons I love tax plans like Steve Forbes is it would greatly minimize the role of the IRS. The IRS falls under the Department of the Treasury. "The first income tax was assessed in 1862 to raise funds for the American Civil War, with a rate of 3%. Today the IRS collects over $2.4 trillion each tax year from around 234 million tax returns."[186] As far as I am concerned the Department of the Treasury is either ill-equipped to provide the necessary oversight or is choosing to allow the Orwellian tactics. IRS representative Lois Lerner pleaded the Fifth Amendment, claimed she lost two years' worth of subpoenaed e-mails and showed great dexterity obstructing truth when testifying before Congress. Sadly, I no longer trust the IRS. Do you?

I want to end this section on Capitalism with some encouraging news. Many believe the euro may soon take the place of the dollar because the euro is the "second-most-traded reserve currency after the dollar."[187] My man Steve Forbes believes the euro is in much the same mess we are in; "The turmoil in Europe is not the result of the euro, but of bad economic policy that combines excessive taxation, overspending, and stifling regulation."[188] "No doubt the dollar has suffered a loss of prestige, but it is still unlikely that it will lose its leadership position in the global marketplace."[189]

We are blessed as "People around the world use dollars because the U.S. economy is the biggest in the world and its capital markets are the deepest, the most liquid and the most innovative."[190]

> The fear that the United States is destroying its traditional advantage with the federal government's high spending and regulatory onslaught is well founded. It is certainly true that the Federal Reserve and the U.S. Treasury Department have badly mismanaged the dollar. But the other major central banks have done no better. For now, the dollar wins by default.[191]

I don't like winning by default, but I do like winning and, "If the Fed continues to taper and scale back on quantitative easing, the United States does not have to be on a collision with hyperinflation."[192]

Proposed Solution

Imagine if Washington, D.C. had the guts to stop spending more than we take in, pull the plug on the presses, quit dreaming up regulation after regulation and relink the dollar to gold. Imagine the Hope and Change that would bring. The stock market would skyrocket as the masses sitting on the sidelines would begin to invest once again. Money would be freed for small businesses to grow and innovators could get back to innovating. Or more simply put, "back-to-basics" should be our nation's rally cry.

"It isn't the gold we have that makes us rich. It's what we make, our know-how, our productivity. So long as this country produces more and better, the world will continue to want what we make."[193]

Malcolm Forbes

PART III

THE PROGRESSIVE ATTACK ON CHRISTIANITY

7

REAL HOPE

I do not pretend to know what lies ahead for our Republic, but I do know that we must not only slow down the Progressive agenda but rid America of its influences entirely. We must honor God, family, and county first not celebrity, technology and the almighty dollar. We are so fixated on cultural concerns our God is often out of sight, out of mind. Nichole Johnson of "Women of Faith" ministries puts it far better that I ever could.

We definitely have a love affair with all things electronic. I'm a gadget girl, too, and certainly not antitechnology, but we are paying a higher price than the one on the sticker for our latest tech tools. They have easily replaced our feelings with facts and our ability to giggle with our opportunity to Google. It's the information not the admiration, what we seem to be after.

Perhaps our culture has simply moved past *wonder*. We're over it. With the onset of globalization, there is less we've never seen and more we've seen too much. Very little takes our breath away, or silences us in sheer awe, or brings us to our knees in humble gratitude for the grandeur we see, if we even see it. There are many closed hearts that are not open to be surprised or delighted. The spirit of the age is "Been there, done that, bought the T-shirt.[194]

Once, when I was on Spring break from college, Mom took me out for a fondue lunch. Enroute to the Swedish café, Mom spotted a Christmas store which happened to be opened year round. She ordered me to make a U-turn and into the parking lot we pulled. My Mother loved Christmas stores more than any other kind of store, so I knew my lunch was going to be delayed for quite some time. I shared her taste in cheese and chocolate fondue, but not Christmas stores. She was excited and acting like a young girl as she walked through the entrance of the shop. I recall her suddenly stopping dead in her tracks and stating; "Sue, it smells just like Christmas in here." She slowly wandered through room after room admiring the many trees each decorated with incredible care and craftsmanship. I was treed out after the first seven or eight. Each tree ornament was special to Mom especially those that showed the Star of Bethlehem, a crèche or the Three Wise Men. Christmas Carols played in each room and Mom hummed or sang to each and every one she heard. She spent over an hour picking out the one special Christmas ornament she would buy for Mark and me to have for our trees once we graduated college and left home. I wandered without purpose behind her bored to death thinking of little but bubbly hot cheesy fondue while Mom continued to lead the way with her face gleaming with awe and wonder.

I spotted a cash register and instantly my spirits soared just knowing the end was near. All of a sudden a Christmas song came over the speakers that sounded like Glenn Miller and his jazz band. Don't you know Mom looked at the woman next to her in the checkout isle, a total stranger, they smiled at one another, nodded, joined hands and did a swing dance for a good five minutes while I melted into the wallpaper. To add to my horror, five or six other shoppers dropped their purchases and purses and joined in the impromptu Christmas dance. My normally-quiet, beautiful mom was the ringleader of the Christmas in spring celebration.

Christmas awed my Mother. Every thought of it was anchored in the birth of Christ. She worked hard to keep Christ predominant in Christmas and Easter. Every day, year round, she would point out a myriad of things to show Mark and me that reflected the wonder of God and His works. Every Christmas and

Easter, Mom made it perfectly clear that all gifts come from God, not Santa Clause or the Easter Bunny, and we must remember to thank and praise Him constantly.

In March of 2012 I was triaged from my doctor's office to the local hospital ER. It was evident to my friend, Ann, and me that I was in very poor condition and that was reinforced when I was wheeled to the head of the line, put in a private room and taken for a CAT scan in a matter of minutes. When a surgeon rushed in and began to tell me of my condition I asked him if I was going to die. He replied, "Sue, you might." Ann and I prayed for my healing, then I closed my eyes and had a private chat with God about meeting Him face-to-face. I told Him I would turn my healing or death over to Him and was at peace. I lay back and began to thank God for he all had given me as I felt very blessed. I thanked Him for my precious family and for friends like Ann and my puppy Luke. I thanked God for the privilege of being born in America and the privilege of knowing Him. I told God that if I was to die I wanted nothing more than to hold my mom, in heaven, and dance with her as she had done at the Christmas store some forty years ago. I was in awe of our God that day and knew, for certain, that what lies ahead is far better than what I was leaving behind. It was on that day that I realized I no longer feared death. I have real HOPE!

Christians know that all of nature speaks to God's existence especially when they hold an infant's perfect little hand with perfectly formed fingernails or watch a puppy play in green grass under a bright blue sky. What is more powerful and awe inspiring than the roar of thunder and the brilliance of lightning bolts? America today has misplaced awe. We must recapture awe and innocence. Our priorities are out of whack.

Attack on Innocence

What happened to innocence? Why must everything today have a sexual or nasty overtone? When you take God out of the day-to-day thought process of living, you reap instead all sorts of feminist and Progressive mumbo jumbo mainly disguised as political correctness. I saw a graphic on Facebook this week that caused me to reflect:

"Political Correctness is Fascism pretending to have manners."[195]

Below is an example of how political correctness is destroying our children's innocence. I chose the story of a six-year-old, out of the many there were to choose from because we are a family of "huggers." Showing affection is a way of life in the Thielke family. Hugs are a perfectly natural act of affection unless...

Schoolyard smooches no reason for child's suspension

Chad Strawderman

Arizona Daily Wildcat

A little kid with thick glasses and scraggly blonde hair got in a bit of trouble a couple weeks ago after his hormones got the best of him. Johnathan Prevette, a 6-year-old from Lexington, N.C., gave a girl a kiss on the cheek at school and was suspended for a day because of it.

The New York Times reported that the school released a statement saying the boy had been "punished not for violating the sexual harassment code, but instead for breaking a rule prohibiting 'unwarranted and unwelcome touching of one student by another.'"

But the school's principal told Mrs. Prevette that "he violated the sexual harassment policy." Mrs. Prevette said the principal gave her the policy and "proceeded to tell Johnathan what he did was wrong. If he was caught again kissing, hugging or hand-holding, he would be suspended."

Although federal education law requires schools to have sexual harassment policies, applying those to 6-year-olds is more than a bit ridiculous...

This entire thing is quite depressing. It illustrates the extreme of paranoia, the backfiring of political correctness. It is proof that society is becoming afraid of affection, afraid of its implications, afraid that a kiss automatically means sex should follow. When was a kiss just a kiss, or was it ever that way?

Lexington's mayor, Richard Thomas, opposed how Johnathan Prevette's case was handled and eloquently stated the solution: "It would seem to be a policy gone awry. The only thing to do is to step forward, admit the policy is flawed, correct it and move on."[196]

Allow me to pose a provocative question. Would any punitive action have been taken had young Johnathan kissed another little boy? I think not. It would be safe to assume that to correct a kiss between two six-year-old boys would be frowned upon as politically incorrect. Attacks on our children's innocence is a plot. An evil plot.

"GLBT" teachers conference in Boston reveals latest plans to push homosexuality even further into schools. Well organized, fueled with taxpayer dollars.

Exclusive report from MassResistance. Coming to your school soon.

POSTED: May 13, 2014

What are the latest homosexual and transgender tactics targeting your schools? In the school "culture wars" nothing happens by accident. It is usually the result of careful planning and execution. Here is a look behind the scenes.

Homosexual teachers, school officials, and education activists (and their "allies") -- along with children as young as fifth grade -- converged at GLSEN's[197] 2014 Annual Conference in Boston last month. At this "hands-on" event they introduced and discussed their latest strategies for thoroughly pushing homosexuality and transgender issues and behaviors into the minds of kids.[198]

Both of the articles above went on and on debating the issues. If these are not examples of the world being turned upside down by Progressives, then what is? Progressives control our schools and are moving to take control over our churches. To minimize the power of the church, the Progressives advocate worshipping at the altar of "whatever feels good."

Non-belief folly

Sin, which is the enemy of the church, is embraced and promoted by the Progressives as a tool to diminish church and parental control. To assist in diminishing God the Progressives embrace and promote a church without God along with all other cults and religions. Progressivism is a religion that worships at the altar of the secular worldview which in turn declares that all religions are really bowing down before the same God. I found the article below to be the most fascinating quoted in our book. How pathetic. Hundreds are weekly venturing off to church without a godhead. The article below is long but it is well worth your time:

LOS ANGELES (AP) — It looked like a typical Sunday morning at any mega-church. Several hundred people, including families with small children, packed in for more than an hour of rousing music, an inspirational talk and some quiet reflection. The only thing missing was God.

Nearly three dozen gatherings dubbed "atheist mega-churches" by supporters and detractors have sprung up around the U.S. and Australia — with more to come — after finding success in Great Britain earlier this year. The movement fueled by social media and spearheaded by two prominent British comedians is no joke.

On Sunday, the inaugural Sunday Assembly in Los Angeles attracted several hundred people bound by their belief in non-belief. Similar gatherings in San Diego, Nashville, New York and other U.S. cities have drawn hundreds of atheists seeking the camaraderie of a congregation without religion or ritual.

The founders, British duo Sanderson Jones and Pippa Evans, are currently on a tongue-in-cheek "40 Dates, 40 Nights" tour around the U.S. and Australia to drum up donations and help launch new Sunday Assemblies. They hope to raise more than $800,000 that will help atheists launch their pop-up congregations around the world. So far, they have raised about $50,000...

...Jones got the first inkling for the idea while leaving a Christmas carol concert six years ago.

"There was so much about it that I loved, but it's a shame because at the heart of it, it's something I don't believe in," Jones said. "If you think about church, there's very little that's bad. It's singing awesome songs, hearing interesting talks, thinking about improving yourself and helping other people — and doing that in a community with wonderful relationships. What part of that is not to like?"

The movement dovetails with new studies that show an increasing number of Americans are drifting from any religious affiliation...

...Sunday Assembly — whose motto is Live Better, Help Often, Wonder More — taps into that universe of people who left their faith but now miss the community church provided, said Phil Zuckerman, a professor of secular studies at Pitzer College in Claremont.

It also plays into a feeling among some atheists that they should make themselves more visible. For example, last December, an atheist in Santa Monica created an uproar — and triggered a lawsuit — when he set up a godless display amid Christian nativity scenes that were part of a beloved, decades-old tradition...

..."The idea that you're building an entire organization based on what you don't believe, to me, sounds like an offense against sensibility," said Michael Luciano, a self-described atheist who was raised Roman Catholic but left when he became disillusioned.

"There's something not OK with appropriating all of this religious language, imagery and ritual for atheism," said Luciano, who blogged about the movement at the site policymic.com.

That sentiment didn't seem to detract from the excitement Sunday at the inaugural meeting in Los Angeles.

Hundreds of atheists and atheist-curious packed into a Hollywood auditorium for a boisterous service filled with live music, moments of reflection, an "inspirational talk" about forgotten — but important — inventors and scientists and some stand-up comedy.

During the service, attendees stomped their feet, clapped their hands and cheered as Jones and Evans led the group through rousing renditions of "Lean on Me," "Here Comes the Sun" and other hits that took the place of gospel songs. Congregants dissolved into laughter at a get-to-know-you game that involved clapping and slapping the hands of the person next to them and applauded as members of the audience spoke about community service projects they had started in LA.

At the end, volunteers passed cardboard boxes for donations as attendees mingled over coffee and pastries and children played on the floor.

For atheist Elijah Senn, the morning was perfect.[199]

The Progressives don't begin to get it. "It" being what we Christians are all about. Our Church is not a building or an hour or two spent worshipping on Sunday. Instead it is every professing Christian, be they dead or alive, since Adam and Eve. Again, church is not a building made by man. It is an institution created by God. Every civilization, no matter where in the world it is located, worships. God put in our DNA a need to worship. The Creator's church cannot be replicated by a gathering of atheists, Progressives or witches. To do so is sheer folly.

Solution

There is a move to attempt to control by legislation what our preachers preach, especially when it comes to abortion and the definition of marriage. There are some things that simply cannot be legislated. To legislate sin is nonsense not to mention evil (abortion, definition of marriage.) As the Progressives press their politically correct agendas, I am confident a sleeping giant will awaken and then, and only then, will they begin to understand how powerful the church is and what we stand for. Christians must live, legislate and stand for The Truth.

In my twenties I went through a stage where a church without rules would have been very alluring. I get it. I believe the godless church goers to be seekers looking for the peace I felt when I faced imminent death. They want to believe way down deep in their souls. They want to know they will see their deceased loved ones again and maybe even dance with them. How sad and lonely it must be to believe our time on earth terminates below ground in a dark, eternal, lonely coffin. Pray for seekers and hand them your copy of this book along with a Bible.

Do we as a culture realize the risk and danger of flaunting God's Word?[200]
James Perry

Security

Recently President Obama has chosen to embrace thousands of illegal aliens who have recently crossed our borders. His circular logic goes something like this: He suggests we give the illegals a road to citizenship "amnesty" and then he will look at the border issue. Talk about putting the cart before the horse! I love Huckabee's take on the immigration issue:

Huckabee Facebook posting July 21, 2014

I've been asked several times what is the Christian thing to do about the tens of thousands of unaccompanied children who have fled to the United States illegally. Let's be clear—there is a Christian thing and there's a government thing. I find it interesting that the same people who scream for separation of church and state now want the government to act like a church and provide assistance and benevolence. Helping the poor and aiding the homeless and the helpless is indeed the duty of the church. But the duty of the government is to protect us—not provide for us. If the border agents are playing wet nurse and changing diapers and beds, then we aren't protected very well. Render unto Caesar the things that are Caesar's and unto God the things that are God's. If Christians would give a dime of each dollar in tithes to fund assistance to the needy, the government wouldn't need to be a big charity.

Government isn't supposed to rearrange people's social standing and redistribute income. Instead of straining social service budgets and education budgets and court budgets in the US, it would be better if our government acted competently and did its Constitutional job to secure our borders. The churches, charities and relief organizations could deliver supplies to those in need around the world. We should be interested in helping the people of other nations experience the fruits of freedom and free enterprise. If they wish to come to America, we should welcome them when they come through the same legal process that we would have to go through to go to their countries. But to not have a border is to not have a brain. We can love people and love security at the same time. But if you give up security, you really don't love the people very much either.

I hope every reader of this book understands the severity of President Obama's no boundary worldview. Porous borders have allowed all sorts of worldviews to set foot on our soil, including many who wish to do us great harm. Radical Islam brought the terror of 9/11 to our shores. Many innocent people died and families were destroyed. From fighting in foreign theatres to expensive security upgrades, especially those involved with air travel and controlling diseases such as Ebola and enterovirus D68, the costs are endless.

Part and parcel of our national security is energy self-sufficiency. President Obama's political hold on the Keystone Pipeline is another example of his NOT doing what the majority of Americans wish, and more importantly, what is in the best interests of our country. He politically favors and owes the "greenies." His kowtowing to the environmentalists keeps the United States at the mercy of the Middle East oil producing countries. Our reliance on foreign oil is nothing shy of resource mismanagement. We should be attacking the Keystone Pipeline and fracking with the same "can do" attitude Kennedy led with to the moon.

Brainwashing

The Progressives proclaim there is one God who is the God of all religions. They believe every worshipper, including satanic cults (devil worshippers), are bowing to the same God. One God-One World is the biggest and most damaging lie perpetuated by the Progressives. The Judeo-Christian God is not the Allah that led the Islamic Terrorists to plow two aircraft into the World Trade Center. In its attempt to eliminate the threat of Christianity, Progressive political correctness, deems all religions equal. Progressives seek to put all religions/beliefs into one big secular-like assembly with themselves installed as the rulers. This form of propaganda is packaged as "fairness," constantly making the point that if one believes his religion is the one blessed by our Creator, then that religion is made up of mean-spirited, anti-scientist, ignorant morons bogged down with phobias. I have been accused of leaving my brain at the door when I attend

Worship services. A proud, condescending PhD friend of mine once laid that on me while we were out to dinner.

Radical Islam is a threat. It is working to exterminate you. The Syrian Bomber, Moner Mohammad Abu-Salha, who committed suicide back in June grew up near my home in Florida. He was raised a Muslim within a few miles of my home. When my neighbor departed for Syria, he was NOT obeying the Judeo-Christian God, nor were the 9/11 or Boston bombers. The beheading in Oklahoma was not in obedience to my God. Of this I am sure.

Please note that our educational system is bending over backwards to accommodate to Islam while taking punitive action against a student for saying "God Bless you" to a sneeze.

US Public Schools Teaching Children Pro-Islamic Propaganda
By Marc Sheppard

Christianity was started by a young Palestinian named Jesus and the 9/11 murderers were not Islamic Fundamentalists but simply a generic "teams of terrorists." That's the caliber of politically corrected crap many of our children are being taught in American public schools -- and it's past time all parents took serious notice.

A five year study by Gary Tobin and Dennis Ybarra of the Institute for Jewish and Community Research cites hundreds of such errors and distortions found in "28 of the most widely used social studies and history textbooks in the United States." Their book, *The Trouble with Textbooks: Distorting History and Religion*, examines the pro-Islamic disinformation they uncovered, including the assertion that Jesus was a Palestinian, not a Jew.

Ybarra claims that the textbooks also treat Islam with special privilege and tend not to criticize or challenge it, as they do Judaism and Christianity. He offers this example from the glossary of *World History: Continuity and Change*:

It calls the Ten Commandments "moral laws Moses claimed to have received from the Hebrew God," while the entry for the Koran contains no such qualifier in saying it is the "Holy Book of Islam containing revelations received by Muhammad from God."

Education expert Gilbert T. Sewall, the director of the American Textbook Council, has also found a decidedly "whitewashed" version of Islam in school history books. Sewall told Fox News that pusillanimous "publishers have been pressured by Islamic activists to portray the religion in the most favorable light, while Islamic terrorism is downplayed or glossed over." He singles out the textbook World History: The Modern World for intentionally omitting the religion of the 9/11 hijackers:

"On the morning of September 11, 2001, teams of terrorists hijacked four airplanes on the East Coast. Passengers challenged the hijackers on one flight, which they crashed on the way to its target. But one plane plunged in to the Pentagon in Virginia, and two others slammed into the twin towers of the World Trade Center in New York. More than 2,500 people were killed in the attacks."

No mention of Islamic Fundamentalists. No mention of jihad. No attempt to explain the identities or murderous motivations of the madmen who perpetrated the most horrific attack on our country ever.

And speaking of jihad, here's how Sewall described what the book History Alive! The Medieval World and Beyond teaches students about the subject:

"Jihad is defined as a struggle within each individual to overcome difficulties and strive to please god. Sometimes it may be a physical struggle for protection against enemies," the book reads, noting that Islam teaches "that Muslims should fulfill jihad with the heart, tongue and hand. Muslims use the heart in their struggle to resist evil.[201]

When I worked for Pan American Airways, I would frequently attend meetings on the upper floors of the World Trade Center. Daily I say to myself, "there but for the grace of God go I" when I think of the awful way nearly 3,000 died. Terrorists know how to do terror, and they work hard at honing their skills. Watching the buildings implode one by one and knowing many leaped to their deaths will forever be etched in my mind. Fighting terrorism must begin at our borders.

Repent – Back to Basics

Most of America is paranoid due to the deluge of lies coming from Washington, D.C. Americans are sick of partisan politics and sick of political correctness being shoved down their throats. Anxiety is at an all-time high. Our kids are seeing abortions, not to mention beheading, on YouTube. Our politicians have 20/20 hindsight and exhibit zero foresight. Blame is the name of the game be it Benghazi, IRS, ISIS or immigration, to name a few. Political correctness has us speaking of beheadings and shouts of "Allah" as "workplace violence," even at our military post Fort Hood.

Progressives are busy taking the name of Jesus out of everything. It is as if they are God phobic. They fail to understand that hell is man's default position, not heaven or a nothingness. Our Founders built man's inclinations into the founding documents which Progressives choose to ignore. It is for good strategic reasons they wish to do away with the Constitution. We **must** cast our votes for men or women who embrace our Founders' wisdom and the Judeo-Christian worldview. Party matters little – character matters lots. We must put our country first and vote to balance the budget and lower our debt for the good of future generations, NOT vote OUR pocketbooks. We must cut the federal spending and the printing of paper money.

Today's special interest groups are not interested in building up every man, woman and child to meet their potential. Instead today's special interest groups are all about ethnicity, gender and standard of living. An equal standard of living for all (unless you hold power and vote to exempt yourselves) is their stump speech.

Sadly, for some time now our commander in chief has been Saul Alinsky. This will continue to be the case in the future if Hillary or a Progressive like her is elected. In my opinion, Hilary's IQ far surpasses Barack's which makes her far more dangerous to America.

8

THE PROGRESSIVE MARK

Celebrity

The first example I remember of celebrity being catapulted to god-like status was O. J Simpson. Remember the O.J. Simpson trial? When O. J could not, no matter how hard he tried, maneuver the glove onto his hand, and his lead attorney Johnny Cochran dramatically proclaimed "If the glove doesn't fit, you must acquit." A stunning piece of theatric attorneying, wasn't it? The dried-up bloody glove was not a game changer to most of America watching the trial at home on their televisions'. The California jury saw the shriveled glove to be a convenient form of "reasonable doubt" and, presto O. J walked out of criminal court a free man. "What began as a double homicide near Santa Monica, Calif., immediately became a media mega-story that would come to be known as the "trial of the century."[202] For over a year, the O.J. saga mesmerized the nation and dominated public imagination. I believe O. J would have been found innocent by that jury, glove or no glove, because The Juice was charming, drop-dead gorgeous, famous, a renowned athlete, well-spoken, cool in demeanor, and, last but not least, a celebrity. O. J, the man, was iconic in his day. He was an idol, a celebrity.

Be it O. J or any of today's abusive NFL players, we have elevated thugs to celebrity. Because of O. J's celebrity, he was given possibly enough slack to murder. Celebrity is as big as it gets in America today. A "selfie" with a star is priceless to the owner:

Joan Rivers' doctor took a selfie while she was under anesthesia, report claims

Joan Rivers' personal doctor snapped a selfie while the comedian was under anesthesia and the physician was about to perform an unauthorized biopsy that led to her fatal cardiac arrest, a report said Tuesday.

The doctor took the photo in the procedure room at Manhattan's Yorkville Endoscopy before performing the procedure on Rivers' vocal cords, according to CNN.

A staffer at the clinic told investigators about the doctor's behavior, the cable-TV network said.

Rivers was at the clinic for an endoscopy to be performed by gastroenterologist Dr. Lawrence Cohen.

Cohen and the clinic's medical director finished their work on Rivers before her unidentified personal physician took it upon himself to perform the biopsy, CNN said.

But before performing the unauthorized procedure, the doctor allegedly pulled out his camera to snap a picture of himself with the legendary star while she was unconscious, according to the network.

It was during the biopsy that Rivers suddenly went into cardiac arrest.

Investigators believe that her vocal cords began to swell during the biopsy on Aug. 29 and the flow of oxygen to her lungs was cut off, CNN said.

She died a week later.[203]

How culturally sick is a doctor who would invade a patient's privacy to procure a "selfie" of himself? Once again, it's all about him, the doctor, not the patient. This selfie may be the most expensive one ever taken by the time Joan's estate is done with him. I wonder what his defense will be?

Now who could forget the smug little punk Ethan Couch, the Texas teen who killed four people in a drunk driving accident who got only 10 years' probation? Because of his rich, elite status, his attorney argued that because he was raised in such affluent circumstances, he failed to grasp the concept of his negative actions and thus couldn't be held responsible for his actions. Never mind that he plowed his car into four people and savagely murdered them. Never mind that after he realized what had happened he ran and left the scene. All that doesn't matter. In the eyes of Texas District Judge Jean Boyd, this teen never faced jail time. Instead, he was given the luxury to attend a very expensive, very prestigious rehab center.[204]

What is going to happen as Ethan and others like him are protected from themselves by parents and a government whose first response to a problem is to throw money at it. In Ethan's case, money was thrown at an opportunistic bottom-feeding attorney scavenging in a system where wealth often wins.

A psychologist called as an expert defense witness said the boy suffered from "affluenza," growing up in a house where the parents were preoccupied with arguments that led to a divorce. The father "does not have relationships, he takes hostages," psychologist Gary Miller said, and the mother was indulgent. "Her mantra was that if it feels good, do it," he said.[205]

It seems all an attorney has to do is play the blame game and his client walks. It sounds so reasonable when blame is cast elsewhere, yet Ethan killed four pedestrians when he lost control of his pickup truck while driving drunk. Prior to the incident, he and his six friends stole two cases of beer from a store whose surveillance cameras nailed them in the act. His blood-alcohol limit was three times the legal limit.

The same article reports the psychologist Gary Miller said with a straight face in court,

"…that the teen was a product of affluenza and was unable to link his bad behavior with consequences due to his parents teaching him that wealth buys privilege."

I would love to know Mr. Miller's fee for testifying. I also wonder if his tune would change had one of his loved ones died at the hands of the dreaded disease affluenza.

Affluenza seems to be going around under different names. It's catchy. Celebrity, even a little, makes people believe they are the center of the universe. Their center of the universe, "it's all about me agenda," champions all others and often becomes totally consuming. It's like the opera star warming up: "Me" "me" "me."

Remember the pro-Obama Sandra Fluke of contraception fame? She is currently campaigning to be a California state senator. Why not since she was the shining feminist star at the December 2012 DNC Convention? Recall the poor Georgetown Law student who testified to the high cost of contraception and how damaging the costs are to reproductive rights. Recently Sandra told the press:

"… the co-eds of Georgetown were going broke because they had to pay a thousand dollars a year for contraceptives. This dire financial need was supposed to trump the religious and economic liberty of her targets."[206] Her target is clearly, Catholicism. When a reporter from CNSN advised her that the Target store, just down the road from Georgetown, sells a month's supply for $9.00 Fluke offered the following excuse; "So, I'm not familiar with specific department store policies."[207] Looks to me like she is only intimate with her game plan and she's sticking to it. To progressives such as Ms. Fluke the end game is all important. Remember Alinsky's, *Rules for Radicals*? The means by which Progressives achieve their goals are irrelevant be they lie, steal or cheat. We live in a very negative hostile world constantly breathing in cynicism because of opportunists like Ms. Fluke.

If you think I am being too tough on Ms. Fluke, I'm not. Most of America, but for the Progressives, would like to see America return to its glorious days of yesteryear. Most of America would like a return to a functioning Washington, D.C. If California elects Sandra, it will be buying someone who hates the other side of the aisle so much she would rather be with Islamic extremists than Republicans. I kid you not!

Speaking on NPR's internet public radio station **KCRW** in Santa Monica, Fluke was asked her opinion on the situation in rural Nigeria, where Islamists are holding around 250 school girls hostage, threatening to sell them into sexual slavery (or worse) if the government does not release numerous political prisoners they want to see freed from jail. Addressing the matter of the radical group **Boko Haram**, which has killed, bombed and kidnapped people before and has the lowest opinion of women, Fluke told KCRW host Madeleine Brand on her afternoon show that the girls being held captive by the militants should "count themselves lucky" they weren't being held captive by Republicans or working for Republican lawmakers.[208]

Good grief. When I write a fiction book, I hope I can conjure up plots this shocking and provocative. California, remember, you get what you vote for. Go to the head of the Progressive class, Ms. Fluke, and take a seat by Hillary. Don't you wonder how long Ms. Fluke's pro-abortion, feminist, liberal worldview would last among militant Islamists before they would behead her just to shut her up?

Progressives worship at the altar of abortion. Doesn't that sound off the wall but:

Cash Cow Abortion

Former Abortion Clinic Owner: We Pushed Sex Ed on Kids to Create a Market for Abortion.

by Nancy Flanders, LifeNews.com

For six years Carol Everett operated four abortion clinics in Texas.

As reported by The Catholic Register, Everett earned a commission for every abortion in addition to a share of the fees charged by each clinic. She says she sold abortion and made big bucks off of the "cash cow" of abortion. A new abortion clinic, she said at the annual Rose Dinner for the National March for Life in Ottawa, would make enough money to pay for itself in a single month.

The clinics' system to make the quick cash was quite simple. The abortionist would move from one room to the next, performing abortion after abortion, often without cleaning up between abortions, according to Everett.

In addition, Everett said that the counselors at the clinics are more like telemarketers. They are trained to schedule abortions and use wording to eliminate a potential clients' fears and objections concerning abortion.

Everett, who left the abortion industry after a Christian business counselor she hired lead her to Christ, also talked about how damaging government-funded sex education programs are. In her speech at the Rose Dinner, **she took aim at the programs for stealing away the innate modesty of children and creating a rift between children and their parents.** She says that the programs aim to teach children that talking to their parents about sex is uncomfortable and then they offer to be the people the children turn to for support. **She says that girls are then provided with low dose birth control, which is ineffective if not taken at the same time each and every day, which is close to impossible for any teenager. When the girls get pregnant, they then turn to abortion clinics, she says.**[209] (bold emphasis mine)

The facts speak for themselves. They entrap girls into an unwanted pregnancy as a revenue-generating marketing tool.

Question: What happens when abortion is considered a comfortable matter-of-fact choice with zero stigma?

Answer: You make a "selfie" abortion and post it on YouTube for the world to see.

Imagine posting a selfie-abortion on YouTube. Consider:

...the latest darling of the abortion-rights movement. Emily wants to proclaim to the world "... that there is such a thing as a positive abortion story. It's my story."[210] "I don't feel like a bad person. I don't feel sad. I feel in awe of the fact that I can make a baby. I can make a life. I knew that what I was going to do was right."[211]

Emily Letts aborted her baby's life while simultaneously casting the image of the defenseless little corpse into eternity using social media. She is stunned and in awe of her ability to make a baby. Emily calls her baby, "her baby", yet allows its precious little warm body to be thrown into a doctor's garbage container. This is too pathetic for words. No doubt Emily will run for public office someday as yet another rising Progressive. If this is progress, I choose to be left in the wake. If Emily ever has children, I pray they never see their mommy's selfie.

Hooray for Hollywood.

Obvious Child: A Romantic Comedy Starring Abortion Coming to a Theater Near You...

...OBVIOUS CHILD is an honest comedy about what happens when Brooklyn comedian Donna Stern (Jenny Slate) gets dumped, fired and pregnant just in time for the worst/best Valentine's Day of her life. Forever nudged by her parents to make better choices, Donna's forced to do just that when a one-night stand leads to a difficult decision that does and does not define the rest of her life. Though confident in her choice, Donna must gain the confidence to believe in her talent, herself, and the best in those around her, especially one surprisingly decent guy (Jake Lacy) who just might make this the worst/best Valentine's Day ever.

So a girl gets dumped, has a one-night stand, and then has an abortion. Sounds super romantic. It's exactly the stuff girls dream of. Maya Dusenbery at Feministing is thrilled about it, Jezebel gushed over it, and the original short film got rave reviews from Bitch Magazine. And they're just so, so sad that more movies don't lovingly feature abortion. Because, you know, that's just what romantic comedies need to up the love factor: some baby-killing. Nothing says love and intimacy like ripping a baby apart limb from limb!

The odd thing about this is that it isn't the first time pro-aborts have felt the need to cram abortion into romantic situations. They've bemoaned the lack of abortions in romance novels, celebrated a wedding announcement that gushed over the couple's abortion, and tried to make abortion romantic in the creepiest abortion ad of all time.

Abortion advocates have been clamoring to link abortion and romance, and are just dumbfounded that it — shockingly isn't catching on.

But why would it? There is no one out there who dreams of the day that they can have their very own abortion. Even pro-aborts will say that women don't make the decision to have an abortion lightly, and pay all kinds of lip service to how difficult and emotional it can be. People read romance novels, or watch romantic comedies, for escapism, to enter a fantasy world for a while, where obstacles can be overcome and love wins in the end. Abortion doesn't fit into that world.[212]

It appears that "Obvious Child" was a box office FLOP, but the liberal reviewers like "Bitch" loved, loved, loved it. No surprise here. I can't begin to tell you how much I have learned from writing this book. I learned there really are magazines titled "Jezebel" and "Bitch." Catchy names, aren't they?

Feminists, especially celebrity feminists, are sure their woes are, shall we say, "World Class Woes." Many who follow them on Twitter buy into the celebrity promotional pity parties:

Gwyneth Paltrow: Reading Mean Comments on Twitter is Like Surviving Bloody, Dehumanizing War

Oh, Gwyneth. First you had to tell "normal" moms that your life is so much harder than theirs because you're a world-famous celebrity. Then you had to "consciously uncouple" from your husband in an online letter announcing your divorce.

We were almost ready to forgive, and then you had to go and compare reading mean comments from trolls online with surviving a war.

via NY Daily News:

"You come across (online comments) about yourself and about your friends, and it's a very dehumanizing thing," the star said. "It's almost like how, in war, you go through this bloody, dehumanizing thing ... My hope is, as we get out of it, we'll reach the next level of conscience."

Really? A war? Please tell that to the nation's servicemen and women, or tell it to the families of soldiers who have lost their lives in battle. Maybe they'll offer to switch places with you for a day so you can see if that comparison is actually appropriate.

There are many celebrities out there like Paltrow who minimize and belittle the sacrifices our soldiers make. But there are bright spots, too – amazing celebrities who use their fame to help and honor our nation's heroes – Gary Sinise, Mark Wahlberg, and Mike Rowe, just to name a few. There is hope yet, but it would be nice if someday, we treat our nation's heroes with the reverence and honor we instead bestow upon movie stars.[213]

Celebrities, including many politicians, seem to believe that just about anything is less important than that in which they are involved. To repeat the quote above:

…it would be nice if someday, we treat our nation's heroes with the reverence and honor we instead bestow on movie stars.

Boo Hoo. Imagine Gwyneth staying home 24/7 raising her two children, Apple and Moses. It appears she is paid far better than the average stay-at-home mom. According to Celebrity Net Worth Gwyneth's net worth is a mere $60 million.[214] Her affluenza has rid Ms. Paltrow of any and all sense of reality.

Comparing mean-spirited on-line postings to going off to war is about as self-centered as it gets.

Perhaps the best response, however, comes from Green Beret and Purple Heart recipient Bryan Sikes. Via Clash Daily:

To Miss Paltrow,

I'd first like to start out by saying how terrible I feel for you and all your friends that on a daily basis have to endure mean words written by people you don't know. I can only imagine the difficulty of waking up in a 12,000 square foot Hollywood home and having your assistant retrieve your iPhone, only to see that the battery is low and someone on twitter (the social media concept that you and all of your friends contribute to on an hourly basis to feed your ego and narcissistic ways), has written a mean word or 2 about you. You've hit the nail on the head, war is exactly like that. You should receive a medal for the burden you have carried on your shoulders due to these meanies on social media.

You said, "It's almost like, how in war, you go through this bloody dehumanizing thing and then something is defined out of it." I could see how you, and others like you in "the biz", could be so insecure and mentally weak that you could pair the difficulty of your life on twitter to my brothers who have had their limbs ripped off and seen their friends shot, blown up, burned and disfigured, or wake up every morning in pain – while just starting the day is a challenge. How about our wives? The ones that sign on to be there for us through thick and thin, that help us to shake the hardships of war upon our return? And do all this while being mothers to our kids, keeping bills in order because we are always gone, and keeping our lives glued together. They do all this, by the way, without a team of accountants, nanny's, personal assistants, and life coaches. Yeah, reading a mean tweet is just like all that.

You know what is really "dehumanizing", Miss Paltrow? The fact that you'd even consider that your life as an "A-list" celebrity reading internet comments could even compare to war and what is endured on the battlefield. You and the other "A-listers" that think like you are laughable. You all have actually convinced yourselves that you in some way face difficulty on a regular basis. Let me be the first to burst your bubble: a long line at Starbucks, your driver being 3 minutes late, a scuff mark on your $1200 shoes and a mean tweet do not constitute difficulty in the eyes of a soldier.

Understand me when I say this: war does not define me. It is a chapter in my life that helped shaped me. Being a husband and father is what defines me. Remember, sticks and stones may break my bones but words will never…be close to what war is.[215]

God Bless You Mr. Sikes, and thank you for your service. After reading your letter Ms. Paltrow must feel as though she has been through every war since time began. Let's hope her sons, young Apple and Moses, do not inherit lack of respect for the military from their mom who obviously lives on the planet Paltrow. Interestingly, Gwyneth named her lifestyle product "Goop!" Back in the day, when we had something nasty stuck to the bottom of our shoe, our dad referred to it as goop. Just saying.

I am not a big fan of rap music, but I would like to shake the hand of Eminem. He is a celebrity that seems to have his head screwed on right.

A United States soldier wrote a letter to his favorite artist, Eminem, asking the rapper for an autograph... Eminem responded but that he would send the soldier an autograph, but only under one condition... that he soldier had to send Eminem one back.[216]

Eminem is a multi-platinum-selling American rapper, producer and actor who has a net worth of $160 million. Eminem knows it's not all about him. He knows it is also about his fans and, more importantly, it is also about honoring our men and women serving in our armed forces. "Eminem spent his youth moving around Missouri with his single mom before settling in Warren, Michigan."[217] Obviously, Eminem's mom instilled patriotism and thanksgiving into her son.

Go Away God

The greatest obstruction to the Progressive utopia is God. The Judeo-Christian God who created heaven and earth must be marginalized if the Progressives are to rule. The marginalization of God was also a major strategy in the Nazi and Communist handbook. Let me show you some of the ways the Progressives are going about replacing our Creator with the religion of political correctness as political correctness is what they adore.

During the 1950s and early 1960s a US Army lesson plan titled "One Nation Under God" listed two objectives: "To help the individual [soldier] to understand the effect of faith in a Supreme Being has had on the origin and development of our country" and "To lead the individual [soldier] to a recognition of the importance of the spiritual element in his training." The fifty-minute lecture to all Army soldiers aimed at proving that "We as a nation are DEPENDENT upon and RESPONSIBLE to Almighty God."

Today, there is a growing concern among former military leaders that the United States military is becoming more and more secular and therefore Godless. In 1998 Kathleen Johnson an Army Sergeant First Class founded the Military Association of Atheists and Freethinkers (MAAF). The group's early efforts included letter writing campaigns reminding public figures such as Tom Brokaw not to use the phrase, "There are no atheists in foxholes."

There are growing indications that the US military is being used as a "social petri dish" to further short term political agendas versus address growing kinetic national security threats from Iran, Russia, China, North Africa and Syria. Recent examples of this accelerating trend include:

• Declaring climate change as a national security priority…

• The repeal of Don't Ask, Don't Tell by the US Congress in 2010…

• The growing restrictions placed upon both military chaplains and those in uniform on when, where and how they may proselytize and pray. The Thomas More Law Center released a video showing members of the US Armed Forces speaking out about the culture of fear and intimidation in the US military that is forcing Christian soldiers to hide their faith.

• The de-funding of the US military as part of the sequestration imposed by Congress. Sequestration led former Congressman and Lieutenant Colonel Allen West, US Army (Ret.) to ask, "So, as we decimate our military, cut retiree and veteran benefits, and cut benefits to our military families, [while] we are arming federal agencies. Why?"

• The changes, over time, to the Rules of Engagement (ROE) that allows our military to function effectively in a hostile environment. Capt. Joseph John, USN/FBI (Ret) wrote, "Two well-known losses of combat personnel are examples of how the imposition of the new and 'dangerous' ROE forced on combat personnel increased the dangerous environment on the battlefield. The first example was depicted in the movie 'Lone Survivor' where the fear of being charged by civilians in the Pentagon with war crimes, if they silenced a hostile Afghan, resulted in compromising an entire operation and resulted in the death of 3 SEALs. The second event, Extortion 17, occurred because the request for suppression fire at a landing zone, that used to be normally approved to allow a helicopter to land in a hot zone, was denied by senior commanders because of the new and 'dangerous' ROE. That lack of support resulted in the loss of 48 military personnel flying on Extortion 17 (those killed included 16 members of SEAL Team SIX, 20 Spec Ops Warriors, 5 helo crew members, and 7 Afghan military allies); Extortion 17 was the largest loss of life of US military personnel in one day in the 13 year history of combat operations in Afghanistan. There have been thousands of incidents over the last 5 years that resulted in casualties that could have been avoided, if the "standard" ROE were being employed.

Each of these issues, and others such as the growing numbers of military suicides and cases of Post Traumatic Stress Disorder, raise a red flag that the US military has lost its character and moral compass.

It appears God has been removed from the soldier, Godlessness is becoming the norm.[218]

How can it be that our brave men and women die while waiting for orders from attorneys and bureaucrats sitting around conference tables far away from the battlefield?

I treasure the small pocket prayer book my dad carried in his leather flight jacket during WWII. It was a source of comfort to him while flying gliders in Europe and is a source of comfort to me now. Had he been wounded, I am sure he would have pulled the tiny little book out of his flight jacket and been comforted by prayer until help arrived or he passed to Heaven. Either way, man needs God. He always has and always will. Progressives have lost their way. Pray for them to come to know Jesus and His ways versus Saul Alinsky and his ideology.

Campus Christian club found guilty of discrimination for requiring its leader to be Christian.[219]

Please understand. I did not go looking for the examples I used in this book. Most found their way to me on my Facebook stream. "Christian bashing" is widespread and must be taken seriously.

Christian club at Chico State University (CSU) may lose its status as a campus group because its requirement that its leaders be Christians violates a state anti-discrimination policy.

The California State University system said asking leaders to sign a statement of faith violates a 2011 executive order which forbids discrimination based on "race, religion, national origin, ethnicity, color, age, gender, marital status, citizenship, sexual orientation, or disability."

But Greg Jao, the national field director for the Intervarsity Christian Fellowship, said the group should be an exception since its leaders' duties are religious.

"Our student leaders aren't like secretaries or treasurers of other organizations," Jao said in an interview with ChicoER News. "They lead Bible studies and worship, things like that."

Liz Wheatley, a team leader for the group, told Campus Reform that the group is not guilty of discrimination because it allows anyone to be a member.

"I think one of the things that maybe people misunderstand is that our membership is wide, wide open," she said in an interview Thursday. "We're very intentionally multi-denominational and multi-ethnic."

Wheatley added that many people involved in the group are not even Christians, but simply curious students.

If the group loses its status as an official organization it would lose eligibility for revenue sharing — which amounts to $300 to $600 of the group's budget — and lose the privilege of hosting meetings on campus for free.

Groups that are not recognized as official campus organizations have to pay up to $500 per week to host meetings on campus.

Wheatley said this cost would likely force the group to have to move many of its meetings to a church — which might stop many students from attending...[220]

Progressives HATE anything Christian. They use political correctness and false "fairness" at any turn to thwart the worship of the Creator of the Universe. I wonder what the Progressives would think of a Christian being forced on them as their "Alinsky" or "humanist" trainer. Forcing a Bible study to be led by an atheist is Political Correctness 101. You get in their face, yell "fairness" often and loud, and you don't back down. The more vulgar and shocking the better.

Imagine defending a university art project composed of the desecration of crosses with condoms.

A Western Kentucky University art professor and her student are defending what pro-life students are calling an act of desecration and vandalism after the student draped hundreds of condoms on top of crosses displayed in a pro-life exhibit.

The crosses were part of a university-sanctioned display by Hilltopper's For Life. A member of the group actually captured student Elaina Smith as she and another person placed condoms on many of the 3,700 crosses. She reportedly told the pro-lifers that the desecration was part of a class art project.

Smith was asked to stop and when she refused, they called Western Kentucky's campus police. The police refused to stop the cross desecration, telling the pro-life students that it was a First Amendment issue.

Smith's project was reportedly for Professor Kristina Arnold's class. Arnold told television station WBKO that she did not disprove of the idea and that she "encourages learning."

"Learning and debating are not always pretty or polite processes," she wrote in a statement to the television station. "Critical engagement with ideas can get messy."

Kristen Hawkins, the executive director for Students For Life, told Fox News that she was shocked that a university professor would condone vandalism…

…"It appears that several WKU officials knew this vandalism would occur, did nothing to stop it, and allowed it to continue," wrote attorney Travis Barham. "Our clients were exercising their First Amendment rights, and it is the duty of WKU officials to protect those freedoms, not passively allow them to be violated."

The Alliance Defense Fund sent a list of eight demands to the university. In addition to a public apology, they also want to know who purchased and supplied Smith with 3,700 condoms. They also want assurances that the student will be punished for her act of vandalism.

"At a public university, 'critical engagement' also involves respecting the free speech rights of fellow students, something Ms. Smith and Dr. Arnold both missed," Barham wrote.

A university spokesman told Fox News that to their knowledge, the incident is closed.[221]

I find acts against Christianity on college campuses especially painful. It is reprehensible for campus police to allow the desecration to continue. That they obey the dictates of the college administration and not the rule of law is loud and clear. The Progressive agenda is to make void any and all teachings of a Creator God in favor of a worldview with secularism or self as the source of worship. We must pray daily that our students are equipped to discern evil and discount the Progressive agenda. Pray they will hold tight to their Christian worldview upbringing or meet Christians later in life who will plant the love of Christ in their hearts. I could not imagine going through life without Jesus and the hope that knowing Him brings.

Here is an example of what might happen when you take a stand for Christianity and Truth. The example I chose comes from England, but it makes little difference. Political Correctness is Political Correctness and Progressivism is Progressivism. Remember, they are working hard to tear down all borders, so it's all one big pie to them.

A school receptionist faces the sack after seeking the support of Christian friends when her five-year-old daughter was scolded for talking about God in class.

Jennie Cain's daughter Jasmine was ticked off by a teacher for discussing Heaven and Hell with a fellow pupil and came home in tears.

After comforting her distraught daughter, Mrs. Cain, who works at the school, sent a private email to ten close Christian friends asking them to offer prayers for the families and the school.

But a copy fell into the hands of Gary Read, headmaster at Landscore Primary School, in Crediton, Devon.

Now Mrs Cain, 38, is being investigated for professional misconduct for allegedly making claims against the school and staff members. She may be disciplined and even faces dismissal.

The case has caused fresh outrage in the Christian community, which fears its members are becoming the most discriminated against people in society...

...Former Tory minister Ann Widdecombe said: 'There is now daily evidence of Christianophobia in this country and it is high time that it was tackled...

...In the Commons, MP Stewart Jackson called for a debate on "systematic and institutional discrimination towards Christians."[222]

Granted, there are two sides to every story. I encourage readers to give extra attention to the footnotes below for more detail. England is one of the most Progressive countries in the world and yet it is known for its tolerance. England is tolerant of Islamic tenants in its schools but notably intolerant of Christianity. It makes no sense to me what-so-ever especially as the Radicals doing the YouTube beheadings in the Middle East are born-and-bred British Muslims. England best wake up or it will find itself under Sharia Law. If you don't believe ask a British Muslim.

Another example of the one-way street called "Progressive":

The New York State Division of Human Rights (DHR) has ruled that the Roman Catholic owners of an Albany-area farm violated the civil rights of a lesbian couple when they declined to host the couple's same-sex "marriage" ceremony in 2012.

Robert and Cynthia Gifford, who own and operate Liberty Ridge Farm in Schaghticoke, were ordered by DHR Judge Migdalia Pares and Commissioner Helen Diane Foster to pay $10,000 in fines to the state and an additional $3,000 in damages to the lesbian couple, Jennie McCarthy and Melissa Erwin for "mental pain and suffering."

Additionally, the Giffords must provide sensitivity training to their staff, and prominently display a poster highlighting state anti-discrimination laws.

The Giffords' attorney, Jim Trainor, told LifeSiteNews that the two-year-legal drama and resulting fines all stemmed from a single brief phone call in 2012 that caught his clients off guard.

"The entire interaction between the Complainants and the Giffords transpired during a two to three minute telephone conversation which, unknown to Mrs. Gifford, was being tape recorded," Trainor said.

"After communicating the fact that they chose not to hold same-sex marriage ceremonies at the farm because to do so would violate the Giffords' sincerely held beliefs (that God intended marriage to be between a man a woman only), Mrs. Gifford invited the couple to visit the farm to discuss handling their wedding reception, which the couple refused."

The Giffords draw a line, Trainor explained, between a ceremony that solemnizes a homosexual relationship and a reception that celebrates the union after the fact. To participate in the former, they argue, would be a violation of their own religious beliefs, especially because marriage ceremonies on the farm typically take place in and around the couple's home, where they live full-time and are raising their two children...

..."They consider the farm their home," Trainor said. "They live there, they work there, they raise their kids there..."[223]

Issues similar to those I have cited tie small business owners up in court for years. Sadly, often they do not have the funds to fight the good fight while Progressives are often funded by liberal action groups or funded with tax dollars. Isn't that a kick in the pants? I have laid out a few examples of Progressive actions against Christianity, but this next one is one of the scariest. The arrogance of the teacher is stunning.

Student punished for saying "bless you."

Kendra Turner was brought up right. She's the kind of kid who says "yes sir" and "no ma'am." She was "raised up right," with good manners as they are prone to say around Dyersburg, Tennessee.

So it was not out of character for Kendra to say "bless you" after a fellow classmate sneezed. But that common courtesy landed the 18-year-old in hot water.

Kendra said she was rebuked by her teacher at Dyer County High School and thrown out of class for violating the teacher's ban on the words "bless you."

The school would have us believe that a child telling a classmate "bless you" after a sneeze somehow caused a classroom commotion so severe it warranted a punishment? It's a good thing Kendra didn't offer her classmate a tissue.

"She said that we're not going to have godly speaking in her class and that's when I said we have a constitutional right," Turner told Memphis television station WMC.

Another student sent the television station a photo taken inside the teacher's classroom showing a list of banned words. Among the censored words are "dump," "stupid," "my bad," "hang out" and "bless you."

She wrote about her incredible story on Facebook. It was then picked up by the MomDot.com blog and then, as they say these days, the story went viral…

…For whatever reason, the school will not explain why the teacher has an issue with the words "bless you." This one is a head-scratcher, folks. But one thing is clear – religious intolerance is nothing to sneeze at.[224]

I want to end this section on a positive note. Mom and my brother Mark prayed many years for me to accept Christ as my personal Savior. I was on an amazing career path and had no time for God. Mom and Mark did not Bible thump or lecture me to death. They simply prayed and lived as Christians ought. I cannot thank them enough for living the example.

9

POST CHRISTIAN AMERICA!

Post-Christian America. How sad is that? The simple act of typing the term "Post-Christian America" breaks my heart. Our once-proud "One Nation under God" has cast the Creator of the Universe aside as if He is of no value.

I Googled "The Progressive Movement."

> …progressivism was rooted in the belief, certainly not shared by all, that man was capable of improving the lot of all within society…

> Progressivism also was imbued with strong political overtones, and **it rejected the church as the driving force for change.**[225] (Emphasis mine)

Today's Progressives honestly believe, with every fiber of their being, that they are better equipped to rule on earth than God. Their goal is to bring down the government as we know it and to do what they must to minimize the influence of the people of God (aka Church.) One of the ways they do this is by making sin public policy.

The 10 Commandments

I tried to write this segment of our book, but my attempts fell far short of Matt Barber's work. Matt refers to his work as a "much truncated analysis" but I think of it as spot on:

Volumes could be penned on the myriad ways in which the central tenets of liberalism violate each of the Ten Commandments. The following is a much truncated analysis:

The Ten Commandments (Exodus 20:1-17):
1. Thou Shalt Have No Gods Before Me.

At worst, liberalism denies the very existence of God in the forms of atheism and secularism, while, at best, it adopts that wonderfully "inclusive"… religious pluralism. Pluralism presumes to give the false gods of false religions equal footing and denies Christ as He defined Himself: "I am the way and the truth and the life. No one comes to the Father except through me" (John 14:6). Liberal "Christianity" falls under this category. It's pluralism with a Christian stamp.

Secular humanism, liberalism's prevailing false religion, denies God altogether and crowns man as king over himself and the measure of all things. "Eat, drink and be merry, for tomorrow we die."

2. Thou Shalt Not Make Graven Images.

We're talking idolatry here. Liberalism is built on it. First, there's literal idolatry (the worship of man-made idols, animals or inanimate objects) enjoyed by our New Age friends. And then there's everything else: pantheistic environmentalism, the idols of "reproductive freedom," "sexual liberation and equality," etc.

Essentially, liberalism worships the created over the Creator. Liberalism also worships the sins of the flesh (see Commandments No. 1, 6 and 7).

3. Thou Shalt Not Take the Lord's Name in Vain.

To deny God is to take the Lord's name in vain. To deny God as He defines Himself is to take the Lord's name in vain. To misrepresent God, to call other gods God or to deny the deity of Christ is to take the Lord's name in vain. Liberalism does this and much more. Many liberals also mock Christ, Christianity and Christians. They revile the exclusive nature of Jesus, His commands and His faithful followers. They hate truth.

4. Remember to Keep Holy the Sabbath.

This one is a bit tricky as it is widely understood to fall under the Jewish ceremonial law, not the moral law – the old covenant, not the new. Christ Himself healed (worked) on the Sabbath. That said, many Christians still view Sunday as the Sabbath and do, indeed, keep it holy. Not all liberals (there are certainly liberal Jews), but liberalism at large denies the Sabbath any significance whatsoever, much less a holy significance.

5. Honor Thy Father and Thy Mother.

Liberalism seeks to supplant parents with "progressive" government. It diminishes parental rights and encourages children to rebel against the antiquated conventions held by mom and dad. It denies that children even need a mother and father and bristles at the "heteronormative" lack of "gender neutrality" inherent within the very words "mother and father." The sin-centered, counter-biblical notion of "gay marriage" desecrates God's design for true marriage and family and is intended to undermine these cornerstone institutions.

6. Thou Shalt Not Murder.

Abortion, euthanasia, "pro-choice," "reproductive rights," "death with dignity." Need I say more? Sacrosanct is the liberal rite of passage for a feminist mother to slaughter her own child in the womb. Fifty-five million dead babies later, liberals continue to worship at the pagan altar of "choice" (see Commandments No. 1 and 2).

7. Thou Shalt Not Commit Adultery.

This means all sexual immorality as identified in the scriptures, to include marital infidelity, fornication, homosexuality, bestiality, incest, et al. Liberalism, it seems, embraces all perversions of God's design for human sexuality. Central to liberalism is moral relativism. When it comes to sex, you can do no wrong because there is no wrong.

8. Thou Shalt Not Steal.

With class warfare as its fuel, liberalism embraces the redistributionist philosophies of Marx and Engels. Liberalism thrives on theft.

Like some completely incompetent and inefficient Robin Hood, liberal government steals from the middle class to give to the poor, thereby ensuring that liberal politicians remain in power and everyone else remains miserable.

9. Thou Shalt Not Bear False Witness.

I give you Saul Alinsky from his Rules for Radicals: "The third rule of ethics of means and ends is that in war the end justifies almost any means." As we've learned from Barack "you can keep your insurance" Obama, that includes lying. Liberals lie. That's what they do. The ends justify the means. Bearing false witness about detractors of liberalism is par for the course.

10. Thou Shalt Not Covet.

Again, liberalism uses man's inherent covetousness as the driving force behind all liberal economic policies. Creating a political climate of economic envy and class warfare gives liberal government the cover needed to take wealth from those who produce and redistribute it to those who don't. Not only does liberalism violate this commandment, liberalism commands its adherents to do the exact opposite. "Thou shalt covet."

As Satan "masquerades as an angel of light" (2 Corinthians 11:14), so, too, does liberalism masquerade as good. It's deceptively packaged in flowery euphemisms and feel-good sound bites that promise "equality," "tolerance" and libertine notions of "social justice."[226]

The Bible says: Gal 6:7 "A man reaps what he sows."[227] NIV

The current state of America clearly reflects what we reap.

Many, but not enough of us are beginning to see the cultural ramifications of NOT putting God first. Don't things quite often feel wrong or unfair? Putting God first means governing and living using the guidelines given to us by the Judeo-Christian worldview. As we learned in Chapter 1, our Founders penned God into the fabric of every document they wrote.

The quote below written by Randy Alcorn might be called the "State of the Union":

- The average American shops six hours a week while playing forty minutes with his children.
- By age twenty, we've seen one million commercials.
- Recently, more Americans declared bankruptcy than graduated from college.
- In 90 percent of divorce cases, arguments about money play a prominent role.[228]

How can it be that a majority of the American people, including many Christians, would freely choose to embrace secular values rather than those of the Judeo-Christian worldview?

What is it we treasure? What is it we ought to treasure?

A Childhood to Treasure

I was born into a culture of respect and civility unlike today's. I was taught to respect my elders, teachers, firefighters, police officers and those serving in our armed forces. Mom taught that if I was ever lost I was to hurry to the nearest police officer and ask for help. She taught me to wave and say "Hello" to every policeman and soldier I saw as a sign of respect and gratitude. Unlike today, police officers were the good guys on TV and in the movies. Television was chock-full of heroes like The Lone Ranger and Superman who saved those in need week after week. No one seemed to tire of wholesome, family-oriented programs like "I Love Lucy," "All in the Family," "Dragnet," "Happy Days," "Mission Impossible" and my favorite, "Laverne and Shirley." We did not have to endure numerous commercials detailing far more than anyone wants to know about erectile dysfunction, incontinence, or drugs.

John Stonestreet of Breakpoint puts it perfectly:

We're not a culture of "The Cosby Show" anymore. We're a culture of "Modern Family." We are told what is now known as the "new normal." By the way that's a basic definition of culture—whatever a group of people considers to be normal. And once normal is redefined, and when good is called evil and evil is called good, we have to take up the task of rebuilding and restoring... And we have to make the case with our words *and* with our lives.[229]

We have a lot of restoring to do. How much f-bombing do you hear when you watch a movie or simply walk through a mall? How often do you hear the Lord's name spoken in vain as if it was just another adjective? It's heartbreaking. I find myself apologizing to God. We have become an abrasive and coarse people.

Ironically, if secularists would open themselves up to America's historical record, their fears would be allayed, as they would come to understand that Christianity undergirds, rather than undermines our freedoms. Indeed, Christian precepts formed the intellectual underpinnings of American constitutional government.[230]

Long ago, President Ronald Reagan defined the nature of political conservatism using the image of a three-legged stool:

(1) Law governed free-market economic practices,

(2) superior national defense system, and

(3) social ethics and laws that reflect the Judaic-Christian heritage.

Ad hominem attacks on those who believe in and promote this stool aside (i.e., the use of "neo-con" or "war mongering"), our nation is at serious risk if any potential or current political leader fosters the significant dismantling of any of these legs. James Nickel [231]

I am thinking Reagan's stool must be wobbly today given the state of our economy, defense systems and civility. Too many of my friends believe the stool is like Humpty Dumpty and cannot be put together again. I remain hopeful and pray for our country numerous times daily.

It's odd, but I cannot recall any of my schoolmates having only one parent. Single moms were not part of the landscape in the 60's or 70's as they are today. We all had fathers who worked, mowed the lawn and took us on family outings. Families ate dinner together every night. If Dad had to work late, Mom would hand my little brother, Mark, and me a carrot and announce dinner would be delayed. She made us feel thankful to have a father that worked late for our benefit so that the least we could do was wait for him and give him a big old welcome when he walked in the door. She built up our dad and ensured we lived within his income. A few of my friends' mothers worked, but most did not. The family unit that was once the heartbeat of American culture is in a state of disarray.

Unlike in physics and chemistry, very few of the findings in the social sciences can be characterized as incontrovertible. But there's one major exception: the impact of fatherlessness on American children. To name but a few grim examples, 63 percent of teen suicides are from fatherless homes; 90 percent of homeless children and runaways are from fatherless homes; and 71 percent of all high school dropouts are from fatherless homes.[232]

Numbers like 90% of homeless children should not go unnoticed. How is homelessness tolerated in America given how much is sent abroad in foreign aid and how much is wasted by Washington, D.C. on projects such as Solyndra?

My parents never seemed to disagree on childrearing as Dad let Mom call most of the shots. Dad never hit me as spanking was Mom's job and one she excelled in. Mom would be considered a child abuser today for spanking our bottoms with her hand. I was never hit anywhere but on my fanny and although I did not embrace it, it never seemed unfair. Today many parents believe it is illegal to spank your child. Check http://kidjacked.com/legal/spanking_law.asp as the site provides state by state statutes as they pertain to spanking and child abuse. Once again, it's not the law that is the issue, it is political correctness. It's the constant eking away of parental rights by the all-embracing, overhead looming, it's-for-your-own-good, Nanny State.

I remember Dad taking me to work with him on Saturdays to give mom a break and to show me off to his co-workers. Daily, my dad would hold my hand, kiss me and tell me how much he loved me. My brother, Mark, and I were raised feeling wanted, loved and tended. Mark and I remain the best of friends today. I could not love him more. Mark works hard at being the wonderful dad he is.

Feminists have engineered standards that they deem define our males. Fatherhood to a feminist is little more than being a walking, talking, blundering ATM. I met Eric Metaxas while working with Chuck Colson and admire his work at Breakpoint:

The problem is that fatherhood has been valued almost entirely in economic terms. People think that if kids in single-parent homes suffer, it's because they miss their dad's paycheck, not his role as a moral and spiritual authority and exemplar.[233]

Today's secular media elite fill our airways with fathers made to look foolish, in dire need of their children's brilliant worldly guidance. I have tired of men being cast as buffoons acting boorish and ill-educated while their twelve-year-olds are cast as worldly geniuses. The feminists and Hollywood have made fatherhood seem clownlike and unnecessary. In my day we watched a TV show called "Father Knows Best," and most of us truly believed our Fathers did know what was best for us. I did not realize it as a child but I do know now, that my dad would have laid down his life for Mark or me just as Mark would for his sons and daughter.

The Real World

I started with Pan American Airways less than a month out of college in the 70's answering their reservation phone lines: "Good morning, Pan American Airways, Miss Thielke, may I help you?" I was thrilled to start at the bottom and have a shot at working my way up. Today's Millennials believe telephone sales jobs are beneath them. They believe jobs like telephone sales are sub-human. Millennials also believe they DESERVE their idea of a perfect job with a Liberal Arts Degree. I worked my way up the ladder by working longer and harder than those around me. One day I received a call from the human resources department asking if I would give a speech at the annual meeting to thank them for their support in helping me climbed the corporate ladder. They called me because I had become Director of Cargo Sales. The position was not only senior, it was in a typically male-dominated part of the airline – air freight. Human Resources was more than willing to write the speech for me, bless their self-gratifying little hearts. It was not a pleasant chat as I informed them that this was the first I had ever heard from the department, thank heavens. Nevertheless, if they wanted a speech I would gladly give an enthusiastic one about the mom who guarded over me and my lemonade stand and the man who took out loans to put me through college and worked hard to put food on the table. Needless to say I never took that particular podium.

As I said, our dad took out loans to send Mark and me to college. Dad and Mom blessed us by putting our education first. They gave up vacations and new cars plus a lot more to ensure Mark and I were given every opportunity. When I graduated from high school, not everyone went to college. Many went to trade schools and many hit the work force straight away. If a young man apprenticed as an airplane mechanic or a construction worker, he was assured a lucrative job for as long as he wished. Both are worthy trades which America needs. Sadly, today everyone is led to believe they should head off to college straight from high school even if they are totally unequipped. Solid training in the trades is almost gone.

I remember taking a subway in New York City, on my way to Columbia University from work in the Pan Am Building. I found myself staring at a large poster with a bold picture of a subway token and stand-out lettering; "ALL YOU NEED TO GO TO COLLEGE." Staring at that poster, I realized, that one needed far more than a subway token to make it in life. I didn't get it then and I don't get it now. We should be sending many of our high school graduates to trade schools or arranging apprentice jobs for them to ensure they will be able to support themselves. Not everyone is equal in his ability to learn. Man, did I just step on a bunch of Progressive feel good toes. Seriously, aren't we better off offering lower-achieving men and women trade school or apprentice jobs instead of literally forcing them into debt only to eventually drop out of college? We are setting many up to fail.

It's not the getting accepted, it's the graduating.

Speaking of students, their debt has become a Progressive tool. Yahoo Finance speaks to President Obama's Executive Order that caps students' federal loan repayment at 10% of their monthly income. Read below to see how the debt may ultimately be transferred to the taxpayer (what else is new?) and how a sharp student can easily scam the system:

> Federal student debt now tops $1 trillion in America, and an increasing number of young people have been defaulting on these loans. Nearly 15% default within the first three years of repayment.

Student debt is now the biggest area of consumer debt in the United States.

The White House says the new executive order will affect as many as five million borrowers, but it will not be available until December 2015.

Yahoo Finance Editor-in-Chief Aaron Task has reservations about the order. "In 20 years the debt goes away if you haven't repaid it all and guess who it goes back to? The taxpayer. And I just don't think that that's going to end very well for the taxpayer. It does give an incentive for someone to make less money because their debt payment is going to be less and they know over the course of time that debt's going to go away," he says.

Yahoo Finance's Lauren Lyster points out that this might encourage students to take out more debt than they normally would. Task adds, "That might be the origin of the student debt crisis in the first place - the availability of credit.[234]

What happened to working your way through college or joining the military then taking advantage of the G.I. Bill? There is no need to plan or save when Uncle Sam is standing at the admissions table with a wad of cash to cover not only tuition but living expenses. I have college professor friends who tell of freshmen students who do not know how to set an alarm clock or locate a particular building or classroom on a campus map.

Supreme Court's Attack on Religious Liberty

In 1997, the Supreme Court passed the infamous Smith decision. It cut the legs out from under the Founders' view of religious liberty. There is no use delving into the details of the Smith case but to say the Court's decision reads:

> So long as the law governed both religious and nonreligious uses, and did not target only religion, the law would be upheld against constitutional challenge.[235]

In other words, freedom of religion is no longer a right as long as lawmakers write laws applicable to all. The repercussions of the *Smith,* one-size-fits-all decision remain enormous and have set the stage for a continuing domino-like effect of anti-Christian legislation.

For instance, a Colorado baker, Mr. Jack Phillips, citing his First Amendment free-speech and freedom-of-exercise-rights recently refused to make a wedding cake for a gay couple. Citing discrimination, the ACLU sued on behalf of the gay couple:

> "We at the ACLU very much support religious freedom, but religious freedom doesn't mean that somebody who has a business has the right to discriminate against members of the public who want to patronize the business," stated Mark Silverstein from the American Civil Liberties Union of Colorado...[236]

The ACLU's argument sounds reasonable and fair at first blush, but what about the religious rights of the baker? Do they count? The judge replied, "This view, however, fails to take into account the cost to society and the hurt caused to persons who are denied service simply because of who they are."[237] The judge ordered a "Cease and Desist" even though Colorado does not recognize same-sex marriages. The rights of the gay couple trump the religious rights of the Christian because, under the Smith Law, civil rights laws pertain to all. The bottom line: <u>Colorado does not recognize gay marriage but forces the baker to recognize gay marriage with his artistry.</u>

As an ex-small business owner, I feel for Mr. Phillips. "'Not all of life is fair,' Phillips said after the commission's decision. 'I will stand by my convictions until somebody shuts me down.'"[238] I am not so sure I would want to eat a wedding cake I had to sue someone to prepare. I believe many in the government have contempt for Christians like Mr. Phillips and rejoice when they take a stand and close their doors.

Something similar happened to my business partner, Ann and me when we owned and operated a real estate office on Long Island in the mid-90s. We were taken before the Board of Realtors because we had the audacity to announce we were closing on Christmas Day and our inventory of listings would be unavailable for showings. We lost! We lost but told every one of our listings and anyone who would listen that we were being picked on by our competitors for choosing to celebrate our religious holiday. Many of our clients were Jewish and respected our decision. They did not want showings of their homes during their holidays and more than understood our position. We turned lemon into lemonade and eventually received an apology from the realtor who took us before the board. He probably just wanted to shut me up as I was frying him in his own oil. I went into that hearing very confident and never thought for one minute we would be disciplined for honoring the birth of Jesus Christ. Live and learn about the Progressives.

At the tenth National Prayer Breakfast in Washington, D.C., Prof. Robert P. George stated that:

The days of acceptable Christianity in America are over, so in order to be a faithful witness to the gospel, Christians must be willing to suffer the costs of discipleship.[239] (Emphasis mine)

He goes on to say American culture no longer looks favorably on Christians, especially if they are vocal regarding abortion and same-sex marriage. "They demand us to conform our thinking to their orthodoxy, or else say nothing at all."[240]

The Professor asked believers to consider how we will react when tested. Will we be like Peter and deny Jesus or will we stand with Mary, His mother, and John, His disciple, at the foot of the cross? Be assured, there will be a price to pay, and none of us will know how strong our faith is until we are tested. We must all pray that American Christians will have the strength to voice and live the Word, no matter the pressure imposed.

Attack on the Eucharist

It seems free speech on college campuses is free for all unless the speech has anything to do with Christianity. Downright stupidity and indecency are often tolerated.

The best example I can come up with is at Harvard, yes, the hallowed halls of elite Harvard, when a "student organization nearly went through with plans to host a satanic ritual in a room underneath the freshman dining hall."[241] The pro-black mass student organization calls itself the Cultural Studies Club of Harvard Extension School. What is a black mass? It is a hateful, obscene ritual used historically to incite violence against Catholicism. It's a low blow to Christianity, a sideshow starring a nude woman playing the part of an altar while the Eucharistic Host is defiled in disgusting ways.

Of course, the Archdiocese of Boston spoke out against the event and many students signed a petition asking Harvard to step up for civility:

> Harvard University did not intervene, but President Drew Faust did release a statement calling the event "an affront to the values of inclusion, belonging and mutual respect that must define our community." She also attended a holy hour at St. Paul's Church in Cambridge, home of the Harvard Catholic Center, which took place at the same time as the black mass was scheduled.[242]

I consider President Faust a first class hypocrite and gutless wonder for not intervening.

The more I wade through campus issues such as this, it appears to me that many college Presidents consider it job one to appease the leftist vocal cultural warriors. According to Harvard student James P. McGlone,

> The calls for university action against the black mass, however, were not motivated by concerns about objectionable ideas getting a hearing at Harvard. Had the event been simply a lecture or discussion of satanic ideas, neither the university's students and chaplains nor the Archdiocese of Boston would have objected in the way that they did. Rather, their objections were grounded in the fact that, quite apart from any ideas being presented at the event, the event itself was so obscene and so "abhorrent" (to use President Faust's term) in its anti-Catholicism and anti-theism as to subvert the goals and ideals of the university, such that people of good will ought not to tolerate its presence in their community.[243]

James McClone is a junior at Harvard College, and Kudos to him for taking a stand. Doubtlessly, his parents are proud, unlike those parents whose children are members of the so-called Culture Club which advocates parading around nude and degrading the Eucharist. Others like myself are concerned with a possible copycat effect.

> Given the precedent set by the proposed black mass, Timothy George wondered if we could look forward to "a public burning of the

Qu'ran," for example, or "a group of hooded Kluxers reenacting a mock lynching next to the statue of John Harvard."[244]

Freedom of speech does not mean that anything goes. Harvard was empowered to prohibit a black mass on campus but chose not to. They chose to err on the side of radicalism instead of decency.

> If a student group wanted to hold a day-long nudist exhibition in the center of campus, there would be nothing wrong with the university intervening in the name of decency. If a group planned a burning of the prophet Muhammad in effigy, the university could again step in to shut down the event, in the name of civility.[245]

The Glorification of Violence, Hate, and Vulgarity

> "Can you kill, Can you run a protestant down with your,'68 El Dorado,
> (that's all they're good for anyway),
> Can you kill, Can you piss on a blond head, Can you cut it off"
> Yolande "Nikki" Giovanni[246]

Fluent and charming "Nikki" is very active at Fisk University in Nashville, Tennessee. CollegeCalc(/) states it costs $31,148 per year to attend and they do not discriminate against out-of-state students. Of course they don't. Arm your kid with a '68 El Dorado and send him to Fisk so he can major in art and emulate "Nikki." Could you imagine the outcry if a white poet wrote the above and substituted "dreadlocks" for "blond?" You can't make this stuff up. It can only be generated by today's ever-increasing political correctness machine. I wonder what "Nikki's" take is on the poor Americans and British who have been beheaded in the Middle-East, England and right here at home. I shudder to think.

If you think our grade school and high school students are insulated from matters other than reading, writing and arithmetic, then please allow me to burst your bubble:

> A California high school history teacher made a jolting statement in the annual school yearbook that's stirring controversy. Spencer Smith, a senior history teacher at Heritage High School in Brentwood, posed for

his yearbook photo as slain Florida teenager Trayvon Martin, dressed in a hoodie and flashing a bag of skittles, according to KTVU.com. The reactions, as might be expected, were mixed.

Most of the parents that weighed in were not in favor of the idea, according to the report.

"I think that's very inappropriate for a yearbook," one mom said. "This is supposed to be capturing the best moments of the year. And all positive things."[247]

Most of the parents did not favor their teacher's using their child's yearbook used as a political platform. Notice that the talk is about the teacher and his agenda, and not about the graduating class of 2014. The teacher is teaching – It's all about me. Look at me in my hoodie. Look at me holding skittles. Look at me expressing my freedom to wear a hoodie and hold skittles. Look at me, me, me, and me! Mr. Smith's agenda has little to do with academia and much to do with indoctrination. Teachers like Mr. Smith are cultural canons spewing their ideology at our kids during school hours.

Attack on Excellence

"A Rhode Island school district that had come under criticism for canceling a night for honors students over concerns that the event would be too "exclusive" is **reversing** its stance."[248] The numerous initial reports all read similar to:

A Rhode Island middle school is canceling its long-running "Honors Night" event for exceptional students, because school officials are afraid its "exclusive nature" will make others feel left out...

Some parents are afraid the change will discourage kids from working harder to try and make the honor list, the station reported. "How else are they suppose to learn coping skills, not just based on success, but relative failure?" asked parent Joe Kosloski.[249]

In the case of Archie R. Cole Middle School, the school administrators eventually acquiesced to the parents' outcry. A local ABC affiliate reported the school's defense. Principal Alexis Meyer and Assistant Principal Dan Seger stated, "...members of the school community have long expressed concerns related to the exclusive nature of Honors Night."[250] Give me a break. Their concerns are to make sure no one's feelings are hurt. It's all about feeling good about ourselves and not about academic excellence. Once again, a thread throughout our book, parents know more and care more about their children than school administrators. Schools once prepared students for the real world which includes all sorts of letdowns and failures. Incentives to work hard and excel were once considered good and positive things.

Be assured, the teachers unions will never give up or relinquish ground. I remind you Progressive teachers believe they know what is best for all mankind which includes our children. If they are thwarted, they will come up with a "Plan B" such as abolishing grades altogether to make everyone feel really equal and good about themselves. We are becoming the United States of self-esteem:

Milwaukee Public Schools makes shift away from letter grades for K-8.

The dreaded F.

Most parents are alarmed by that letter on a child's report card. But they won't see it this year in Milwaukee's K-8 and elementary schools, as the district does away with traditional letter grades in favor of a new scoring system that separates academic progress from social skills.

In doing so, Milwaukee Public Schools joins a growing number of districts that are eliminating traditional letter grades or untethering student behaviors from academic marks.

The changes — which can include no longer docking points from academic grades for late assignments and offering students multiple chances to submit their work — are a big shift for some teachers, and a head-scratcher for many parents

"I think (district administrators) want letter grades to go away because they want to blur the line of failing students," said Sara Andrea-Neill, a parent in the Kenosha Unified School District.

Administrators say the changes capture a more nuanced picture of a student's academic progress. They also align with the push schools are making to implement the Common Core, a set of nationwide academic standards voluntarily adopted by most states that raise the bar on what students should know and be able to do in core academic subjects.[251]

Most of the parents probably don't really know what is going on. Google "**Common** Core" and take a good hard look at the curriculum that is being taught in our schools. Common Core is mass collectivism on the scale and level of the Union of Soviet Socialist Republics at its height. It will make my examples of overreach look like child's play.

I am not picking on Milwaukee. In the example below, Virginia is also camouflaging failure:

At West Potomac High School - taking F off the grade books.

Depending on whom you ask, West Potomac High School's latest change to student grading is either another sign of a coddled generation or a necessary step to help struggling kids.

The dreaded F has been all but banished from the grade books. The report cards that arrived home late last week showed few failing grades but instead marks of "I" for incomplete, indicating that students still owe their teachers essential work. They will get Fs only if they fail to complete assignments and learn the content in the months to come.

The change in educational philosophy is intended to encourage students to continue working toward mastery of material rather than accepting a failing grade and moving on. Schools throughout the Washington area and the nation have made other moves to improve grading methods, especially as they affect low-performing students, though few have gone so far as West Potomac High, in the Alexandria section of Fairfax County.

"It's a huge paradigm shift," said principal Clifford Hardison, who recalls that when year-end grades were tallied last June at West Potomac, he counted nearly 2,000 Fs, with a large group of teens racking up more than one failed course.

The new strategy has critics - both within West Potomac and beyond - who fear that reducing the possibility of outright failure gives teachers less leverage while also giving students unrealistic expectations about the adult world they soon will enter. Some worry that the reordering of deadlines and test opportunities will also affect the transcripts of the college-bound, giving some students an advantage.

Mary Mathewson, an English teacher, says a number of her colleagues are "livid" about the grading change, which "takes away one of the very few tools we have to get kids to learn." The possibility of failing is a motivator, she says, and now "kids are under the impression they can do it whenever they want to, and it's not that big of a deal."

In the first quarter, half of Mathewson's grades for two 10th-grade English classes were incompletes. "I don't believe it's an extra chance," she said. "It's an out. The root problem is motivation. The root problem is not that we're not teaching them.[252]

Think of the impact on the smarter students. I believe a future employer will care if a new hire is able to catch on quickly or is a laggard. Does anyone care that a slower student may be granted a job over a better achiever because the grading system was based on "feeling good" instead of excellence? Actually, most Progressives would prefer the slower student be hired, figuring the smarter one will find his way.

One more example of cloning mediocrity: Does 50% on a test mean you got half correct?

Broward schools should punt idea to dump zero grades.

April 27, 2013|Sun Sentinel Editorial Board

What a difference a day makes.

On Thursday morning, Broward Schools Superintendent Robert Runcie strongly supported a proposal that would eliminate the grade of zero, making 50 the lowest score a teacher could give, as a way to motivate struggling students to remain on the road to graduation.

"My personal view is, I am in support of it and this is the reason: We are in the business of helping students to be successful and not necessarily having students fail," he told the Sun Sentinel Editorial Board. "It's not right to put any student in a situation that he cannot recover from. With too many zero grades, at some point, you do the math and a student will say, "There is nothing I can do.""

By that evening, Runcie changed his tune. He called back to say the district is still evaluating the proposed change. "There are definitely pros and cons on both sides and we haven't made a determination on where we are going."

Credit Runcie for reconsidering a bad, if well-intentioned, proposal that sends the wrong message about accountability and rewards students just for showing up.

The reasoning behind the push to make 50 the new zero, which surfaced during a school board meeting this week, is that other letter grades carry a 10-point scale, so the range for an F grade should be raised to 50-59, not 0-59.

Proponents believe raising the floor will boost graduation rates and reduce drop-out rates.

By that thinking, so would dumping grades all together.

Changing the yardstick is like giving a trophy to every player, whether or not his team wins the game. It would send the wrong message to students who work hard to make the grade. It's like telling a student, "Don't worry about turning in your homework, Johnny. You'll still earn at least a 50..."

...No doubt, prospects look bleak once students dig themselves a deep hole. For an educator, it must be tough to motivate students who find themselves in such a fix. But is the solution to change how we score their performance? Is that the life lesson we want to deliver?

In this era of high-stakes testing, school accountability and teacher pay based on student performance, Broward's proposal to change the bell curve doesn't pass the smell test.[253]

The decision reached is ill conceived and illogical. The teacher stated, "We are in the business of helping students to be successful..." Wrong, Teachers are in the business of teaching - teaching children the tools necessary to make it in life. Those tools would include arithmetic so they can learn to set an alarm clock and basic map reading skills so they can find their way to a job interview or around a college campus. Their heads need not be filled with liberal politics by teachers wearing hoodies and munching on Skittles. More time should be spent teaching history, reading, writing and arithmetic, and less time should be spent conjuring up grading systems that falsely reflect student and teacher capabilities.

Promoting Vulgarity

Here is a doozy. In Bellingham, Washington the KOMO News Network reports:BELLINGHAM, Wash. -- A Bellingham High School drama teacher has issued a formal apology after her awards ceremony devolved into an evening of profanity, jokes about a priest having sex with kids, and a box of sex toys.

A parent attended the ceremony in the school auditorium with her 17-year-old daughter, who was nominated for an award. Both want to remain anonymous until after graduation on June 6.

The teacher is Teri Grimes, a veteran of three decades who is slated to retire after this year.

In an email to KOMO News, the upset mother complained about the teacher's use of profanity during the ceremony. She said Grimes repeatedly used inappropriate words and told a distasteful joke.

"I sat there with my mouth open in shock and the final straw was when a joke was told on stage about a teacher, a lawyer and a priest on a plane. The plane was going down and the teacher says we have to save the children. The attorney says "F*** the children!" and the priest says "OOOOH...Do we have time for that?" the email reads.

The parent, who brought her young daughter to the ceremony, decided to leave after hearing the joke.

In addition to what she considered offensive language and the off-color joke, the parent said the awards handed out during the ceremony weren't appropriate for children. She said one of the categories was for "the horniest stud," where the award was a sex toy.

"WE need to get the word out there that THIS is the kind of TRASH that is being taught in our schools. I am so shocked right now I am in tears," the parent said in her email to KOMO.[254]

The teacher later apologized but, sadly, the damage was done. Neither the teacher, Teri Grimes, nor any of the students faced any disciplinary action. It was a win for the liberal secular Progressives. Do you really believe Ms. Grimes has repented of her activities and will no longer act in a vulgar manner? I remind you, the Progressives view truth only in light of their agenda. Believe me, no card carrying Progressive is ever going to pass up a chance to bash the Catholic Church.

Attacked by the Media

The media elite are as controlling and stifling to Christianity as are our colleges. Recently, the Benham brothers, who were to host a renovation show on HGTV, were pulled from the programming because of remarks they made during a 2012 prayer rally. No doubt, HGTV would agree to build the scenery for a black mass to be held in the deified, sacred grounds of Harvard yet terminate two young Christian men for hosting an annoying prayer service. The prayer service drew 9,000 attendees calling the church to repentance. The Benhams stand by their prayer rally knowing they are in lock step with Biblical Truth. David Benham stated recently:

> What really happened here was when we were announced in New York City…that's when the Right Wing Watch and GLAAD (formerly the Gay and Lesbian Alliance Against Defamation) decided we're going to go on a smear campaign and try to bully HGTV into firing these guys, and they won. They actually succeeded.[255]

Yes, they actually succeeded. The Right Wing Watch won because they yelled the loudest for <u>their</u> rights while deeming rights to views contrary to theirs as mean-spirited, racist and intolerant. I remind you, The Right Wing Watch espoused they stand for "tolerance."

I predict that the Benham boys are going to carry the day. They are not going to go down without a fight. They know and proclaim:

> The way of Christ is the way of truth, and it's that way that affords everyone in this nation the liberty to believe how they want to believe and to voice it… We're just tired of getting pushed around. We're speaking for millions of people.[256]

These two young men can speak for Roger and me any day. Notice they do not claim to be victimized. They are up to the battle.

One Way Street

What happens when a Progressive sees the light and no longer agrees with the party line?

Fired for 'Diverging' on Climate:

Progressive Professor's fellowship 'terminated' after WSJ OpEd calling global warming 'unproved science'

Professor's fellowship 'terminated' after WSJ OpEd declaring 'the left wants to stop industrialization—even if the hypothesis of catastrophic, man-made global warming is false'

Climate Statistics Prof. Caleb Rossiter: 'If people ever say that fears of censorship for 'climate change' views are overblown, have them take a look at this. Just two days after I published a piece in the Wall Street Journal calling for Africa to be allowed the 'all of the above' energy strategy we have in the U.S., the Institute for Policy Studies (IPS) terminated my 23-year relationship with them...because my analysis and theirs 'diverge.'

IPS email of 'termination' to Rossiter: 'We would like to inform you that we are terminating your position as an Associate Fellow of the Institute for Policy Studies...Unfortunately, we now feel that your views on key issues, including climate science, climate justice, and many aspects of U.S. policy to Africa, diverge so significantly from ours.'[257]

The poor guy was fired for telling the Truth which he had determined in his studies. It's their way or the highway. Progressives have no time for give and take. If you don't believe me, check how many bills have died on Harry Reid's desk since President Obama took office:

... according to Rep. Marsha Blackburn (R-Tenn.), the House has passed a bevy of bills that are sitting on Harry Reid's desk in the Senate.

How many bills? Blackburn told TheBlaze that 356 bills made it through the House and are languishing in the Senate.

Additionally, according to the congresswoman, 98 percent of those bills were passed with bipartisan support. She also pointed out that 200 of the bills were passed in the House with unanimous support from the entire chamber and more than 100 were passed with 75% support of House Democrats.[258]

I wish America knew how many bills Harry Reid has killed. We don't have a do-nothing Congress. We have a bunch of powerful men holding the country hostage to their agenda. There is profit in chaos and propaganda and Harry has been having a field day with jobs bills and pipeline bills, to name a few. The grumpy, stale, career bureaucrat has done great harm to our country. He is ineptocracy personified.

Ineptocracy_(in-ep-toc'-ra-cy) - a system of government where the least capable to lead are elected by the least capable of producing, and where the members of society least likely to sustain themselves or succeed, are rewarded with goods and services paid for by the confiscated wealth of a diminishing number of producers.[259]

Our elected officials are to represent the American people not a political elite driven ideology. How do you like the fact that they have exempted themselves from ObamaCare? What about voting themselves pay raises while jobs bills are rotting on Harry Reid's desk, not to mention generous vacation time and lifelong pensions? Their approval ratings speak loudly.

Eric Metaxas' book, *7 Men and the Secret of Their Greatness*, is about what makes great men truly great. A quote from one of his many positive book reviews indicts many in Washington, D.C. The quote below deals with George Washington.

Starting with the Indispensable Man, George Washington, Metaxas highlights the challenges each faced in life, but particularly the temptation of embracing personal success at the expense of what is right. What sets these men apart is their willingness to walk away from obvious personal gain, to sacrifice for principle and the greater good. Washington, having defeated the most powerful military in the world, did something unthinkable: he walked away from power. King George III remarked that if Washington truly gave up the opportunity to rule he would be "the greatest man in the world.[260]

"...to sacrifice for principle and the greater good" sure doesn't sound like the works of the many men and women in gridlocked Washington, D.C. today.

America Without Christians

Professor George puts it shockingly simply:

> To be a witness to the Gospel today is to make oneself a marked man or woman. It is to expose oneself to scorn and reproach. ... To place in jeopardy one's security, one's personal aspirations and ambitions, the peace and tranquility one enjoys, one's standing in polite society. ... One may in consequence of one's public witness, be discriminated against, denied education opportunities and the prestigious credentials they offer, one may lose valuable opportunities of employment or professional advancement, one may be excluded from worldly recognition ... [being faithful to the Gospel] may even cost one treasured friendships, may.. produce discord and alienation from family members.[261]

Pastor Roger Ball will end our book by addressing Saul Alinsky's *Rules for Radicals* – the Progressive's bible. Pastor Balls work will enrage you and make you cry. Both Roger and I believe our great country is teetering on a precipice. Progressivism is pushing hard while Christianity struggles to hold the line. We must push back and push back with confidence.

PART IV

THE FIRM
FOUNDATION

10

PRICE TAGS, FOG
AND THE CHURCH

Tony Campolo tells an intriguing story at conferences and in his book, "Who Switched the Price Tags?" It seems that as Tony grew up in Philadelphia there was a tradition on the night before Halloween. It was known as Mischief Night, and the key was to find a way to "prank" your friends and neighbors.

Tony and his friends would often sit around and talk about one prank in particular that they wanted to pull off. It would require that the boys finding a way into the Five and Dime store in their neighborhood late at night while it was closed. Once in the store, they wouldn't cause any destruction or steal anything. Instead they would go throughout the store switching the price tags on items. The boys would laugh over the confusion the next day as the store opened. Shoppers would find that toasters were now selling for 25 cents, and paper clips would be $10 apiece. You could buy a flashlight for a nickel, but a candy bar would cost you $15.

I am pretty sure that Tony and his gang never actually pulled this caper off but simply enjoyed the amusing thoughts of how people would respond. On the other hand, I am certain that someone has pulled off a similar scheme on the greatness of America.

For the first three quarters of this book, Sue has laid out a candid and straightforward case for the "serfing" of America, where the casualties of this culture war have been the things that once were considered great in America, like a love for God and country, an unashamed patriotism and an insistence upon personal responsibilities. There was a time when citizenship meant something more than a free piece of paper to get more votes as a politician.

Today many of us stand in the store called America and cry out, "Who switched the price tags?" Just consider the stock of America which once held high value in this nation and what has happened to the price tags on marriage, family, a strong work ethic, honoring those in leadership, church - and the list goes on. Progressivism is destroying a sense of value for these things. Instead we have placed high price tags on sex, sexual preference, and those things which feed our unlimited appetites for sensual pleasure. Turtle eggs carry an almost unaffordable price tag while human embryos are disposable matter today. We now value the "flip the fault game" whereby we find someone to blame for our own risky behaviors and the poverty that ultimately results. We place value on destroying reputations and tearing apart the engine of commerce that grew this nation into not only the most powerful country in the world, but the most benevolent by far. No other nation matches the help that comes from America in times of crisis. But if Progressives get their way, that engine will be dismantled and the government will be the producer of wealth. Few seem to see the problem with that scenario. The government cannot produce wealth; it can only consume it.

The community in which I live, Vero Beach, FL, is a prime example of limiting the engine of commerce. Powerful political groups in our community work tirelessly to keep commerce away so that we might remain a quiet little bedroom community. As a result, the largest employers are now various forms of local governments. As a result, the community has now earned the scandalous distinction of being the number one city in America for disparity between the very rich and the very poor. The middle class in our community is a dying breed, headed for extinction.

Additionally, throughout our nation, many seem bent today on erasing, or at least blurring, the lines that once clearly directed our moral path in America.

Our founders relied upon two documents as a moral compass to lead this nation. One was the Constitution and the other the Bible. Today we find more and more who hold the notion that, "that was then, and this is now." Both the Constitution and the Bible are being dismantled by Progressives as inadequate, antiquated and irrelevant. While the former will ultimately in time cease to exist, the latter will not. The Bible is an eternal document with God as the author and the power of God as the Sustainer. Here is what God spoke through the prophet Isaiah concerning the Word of God: **"***The grass withers and the flowers fall, but the word of our God stands forever"* (Isaiah 40:8). Jesus said that heaven and earth would pass away, but His words would not pass away (Matthew 24:25). Yet the more we seek to ignore the Founders commitment to Judeo-Christian values as a moral compass and replace it with a carefully crafted agenda of socialist values, the more confusion will reign and the more the chaos that already plagues our cities, our schools and our workplaces will increase.

One of my favorite instruments to talk about on an airplane is the gyroscope. In the early days of flying, it was an actual gyroscope that would help the pilot determine the level flying of the airplane. One of the important benefits this amazing instrument offered was that it clearly let you know if you were flying upside down in a fog, headed for sure disaster. Once the value of this tool was realized, no self-respecting pilot would take off without it, and ultimately it became required instrumentation.

For over two centuries the Constitution and the Bible were the gyroscopes of the culture in America. They guided our nation through many a conflict and trial and through many times of crisis. Today our "pilots" are arrogant enough to think that they don't need these gyroscopes. They do as they "feel," ignoring the possibility of torpedoes, and proceed full steam ahead. Now we are flying in a fog upside down and most don't even know it. The only question that remains now for the passengers on this flight is, which will come first, a return to time-proven values, or an impending crash?

Can Anyone Find the Church in this Fog?

I grew up in the mountains of southern West Virginia in a day when summer meant I woke up in the morning, got dressed and then went outdoors for the rest of the day, only returning when I heard Mom's voice beckoning me home for dinner. Being inside in the summer was the worst form of punishment. We played baseball with large tree limbs and rocks. We drank from the water hose. Mom didn't worry about me getting into trouble because all the neighbors had her permission to straighten me out if they saw me doing anything wrong. Getting spanked by a neighbor was not a bad thing, especially since it meant they probably wouldn't tell Mom or Dad…another bullet dodged. Video games were a long way off, and except for 4:00 P.M. daily when American Bandstand came on, the three television stations we picked up from the antennae on our chimney offered little attraction.

My mom and dad had been childhood sweethearts growing up in the hills of Kentucky. They married in their mid-teens and stayed married until death did they part in 1982, when my dad, walking up the steps of church on a Sunday morning, sat down and told someone he couldn't catch his breath. They helped him to the Pastor's Study and called an ambulance. He died before the ambulance arrived. Seven years later my mom would join him in death while hosting a ladies' slumber party for the church. She went home to be with the Lord and Dad that night in her sleep.

It probably won't surprise you then that as a child I grew up with a "good" drug problem - good, because Mom and Dad drug my sister, Kathy, and me to church nearly every time the doors opened. Now I am not saying that I didn't eventually stray from the church once I was able to make my own decisions, but I am saying that I am eternally thankful to have had parents who placed a high price tag on the value of training up a child in the ways of the Lord. One of my major concerns today is parents who say, "Well, I don't want to make my child go to church because they may resent it." Or this one, "I'm going to let my children make their own decision about religion." I don't always do it, but I want to say, "Then I suppose when they are running a 104 degree fever and have turned a nice shade of blue you won't be making them go to a doctor since they might resent it later?" My Mom and Dad invested their lives into us and brought us around countless others in the church who invested their lives in us as well. For millennia before Hillary Clinton used the phrase, "It takes a village to raise a child," the church has been the greatest village on earth for raising children.

When I was 14, the Minister of Music at our church started a youth choir that turned into an amazing movement of God for the next four years of my life. The Sounds of Conviction, as we were known, grew from a small youth choir to a full stage production featuring the voices of over 150 teens and a band/orchestra that performed some of the very first contemporary Christian musicals in schools across three states. This was no small feat for a church of less than 200 people in a town of only about 8,000. It was during this time that I am quite sure I heard God's call on my life to preach. However, for a lot of reasons that seemed to make perfect sense to me at the time, I let other voices and other passions drown out God's voice in my life, ultimately walking away from church attendance for several years. In 1982, upon the news of my Dad's death on the steps of church, I awoke again to the foundation of Christ and all that others had invested in me. You might say my temperature hit 104 and I headed for the doctor. Nine years later I would find myself face down at an altar in Ft. Lauderdale, FL, confessing that I had forsaken my first love, just as the charge was made against the church at Ephesus in Revelation 3. The next day I came home, walked away from an advertising and public relations firm I had built from the ground up and waited for God to show me my next step. In a matter of months I was on staff as the Youth Pastor of the church I still serve today.

In those early days of being a Pastor I was naïve enough to think that being in ministry was going to be a cakewalk compared to my corporate experience where it so often was a dog-eat-dog, rat race that drained you daily and challenged you from every corner. It didn't take long for me to see the church in a different light, frankly not a light I expected or liked at first. Somebody once told me that sheep are among the most stupid of animals on the earth. Is that why the Bible refers to us as sheep?

Now, 23 years later, I love the church with all her faults and all her failures. I love the sheep, for I, too, am a sheep under the Great Shepherd, Jesus Christ. When asked what problems we have in our church, I say, "We don't have any problems in our church, just many opportunities to see God at work in the things we cannot fix or do on our own." While I love being the Pastor of Freedom Church and a spiritual leader in our community, I am deeply concerned about the church today in America. The fog that our country is in has had a serious impact upon the church, especially over the last ten years, and rather than affecting the fog as we have been called by God to do, the fog is affecting our vision. No doubt blurred vision will ultimately cause you to veer off course.

Each year that passes the evidence of this veering off the path grows. Consider these statistics from the US Census Bureau Office:[262]

- Every year an average of 4,500 churches close their doors in America
- For decades at least 1000 new churches started each year-but that statistic has dropped in half
- Every year 2.7 million church members fall into inactivity
- During the decade of the 90's the US population grew by 11%-yet membership in Protestant Churches in America dropped by 9.5% overall
- In 1900 there were 27 churches for every 10,000 people in America. Today there are only 11 churches for every 10,000 people

According to the Francis A. Schaeffer Institute of Leadership Development, "The United States now ranks third (3rd) following China and India in the number of people who are not professing Christians; in other words, the U.S. is becoming an ever increasing 'un-reached people group.'"[263] In addition, half of all churches in the US did not add any new members to their ranks in the last two years.

As the fog gets heavier, the news get bleaker. Consider the statistics on pastors in America as reported by the web site PastorBurnout.com:

- 13% of active pastors are divorced.
- 23% have been fired or pressured to resign at least once in their careers.
- 25% don't know where to turn when they have a family or personal conflict or issue.
- 25% of pastors' wives see their husband's work schedule as a source of conflict.
- 33% felt burned out within their first five years of ministry.
- 33% say that being in ministry is an outright hazard to their family.
- 40% of pastors and 47% of spouses are suffering from burnout, frantic schedules, and/or unrealistic expectations.

- 45% of pastors' wives say the greatest danger to them and their family is physical, emotional, mental, and spiritual burnout.
- 45% of pastors say that they've experienced depression or burnout to the extent that they needed to take a leave of absence from ministry.
- 50% feel unable to meet the needs of the job.
- 52% of pastors say they and their spouses believe that being in pastoral ministry is hazardous to their family's well-being and health.
- 56% of pastors' wives say that they have no close friends.
- 57% would leave the pastorate if they had somewhere else to go or some other vocation they could do.
- 70% don't have any close friends.
- 75% report severe stress causing anguish, worry, bewilderment, anger, depression, fear, and alienation.
- 80% of pastors say they have insufficient time with their spouse.
- 80% believe that pastoral ministry affects their families negatively.
- 90% feel unqualified or poorly prepared for ministry.
- 90% work more than 50 hours a week.
- 94% feel under pressure to have a perfect family.
- 1,500 pastors leave their ministries each month due to burnout, conflict, or moral failure.
- Doctors, lawyers and clergy have the most problems with drug abuse, alcoholism and suicide.[264]

With statistics like this, is it any wonder that in the "Progressive"-ly increasing fog in our country, it is getting more and more difficult to find the true church which once was a lighthouse in our nation?

Who Turned out the Lights?

In Matthew 5 Jesus makes a declaration to His followers which goes to the very core of their mission and purpose on earth. Let's examine that again today in view of the obscuring of the church by this Progressive fog.

You are the light of the world. A city on a hill cannot be hidden. Neither do people light a lamp and put it under a bowl. Instead they put it on its stand, and it gives light to everyone in the house. In the same way, let your light shine before men, that they may see your good deeds and praise your Father in heaven. Matthew 5:14-16 (NIV)

Jesus was telling His followers of that day, and of today --- You are the light that shines in the fog. You are to put it out there for everyone to see. Don't be intimidated by religious or political correctness. Welcome being called names because of Me. After all, Jesus was called quite a few names. Don't worry about losing friends on earth. Stop shrinking like a violet because you're afraid of what man might do to you. Shine! I mean it, shine!

Before the American colonies officially proclaimed themselves to be a sovereign nation in 1776 through the Declaration of Independence, this new land had to be discovered and then it had to be settled. Columbus did the discovering; and the settling was begun by the Spanish at St. Augustine, Florida, in 1513. As Spain explored the American south and southwest toward the Pacific Ocean, in 1607, the first British colony was established at Jamestown, Virginia. This first colony was established by Charter under King James for purposes of establishing British claim to the new world, exploration and finding gold. This colony nearly failed and was at the point of abandonment when a supply ship arrived, the people began to survive and a new cash crop, tobacco was discovered. There was not any gold to find but the soil was rich for farming and the plantation era began. Entrepreneurs came to the New World.

In 1620, another group of British subjects landed in Plymouth, Massachusetts, seeking to escape religious persecution. They were known as the Pilgrims. It was these dedicated servants of God who laid down the first order of the Biblical Church of Jesus Christ in America. It's vital for us to understand how and why we were originally established in this land. Though mostly erased from the history books of American public schools, these Pilgrims were unashamed as to why they came to settle this land. They would be so far away from political correctness today that I can only imagine the barrage of ridicule and shame they would face from today's media as they boldly and courageously proclaimed in the Mayflower Compact:

In the name of God, Amen. We, whose names are underwritten, the loyal subjects of our dread Sovereign Lord King James, by the Grace of God, of Great Britain, France, and Ireland, King, defender of the Faith, etc.

Having undertaken, for the Glory of God, and advancements of the Christian faith and honor of our King and Country, a voyage to plant the first colony in the Northern parts of Virginia, do by these presents, solemnly and mutually, in the presence of God, and one another, covenant and combine ourselves together into a civil body politic; for our better ordering, and preservation and furtherance of the ends aforesaid; and by virtue hereof to enact, constitute, and frame, such just and equal laws, ordinances, acts, constitutions, and offices, from time to time, as shall be thought most meet and convenient for the general good of the colony; unto which we promise all due submission and obedience.

In witness whereof we have hereunto subscribed our names at Cape Cod the 11th of November, in the year of the reign of our Sovereign Lord King James, of England, France, and Ireland, the eighteenth, and of Scotland the fifty-fourth, 1620.[265]

Did you read that? The mission, the purpose of settling America, was for God's glory and for the advancement of the Christian faith. The very core of the start of our nation was by and for the church, that it would be a light shining in this new and dark land.

William Bradford, who made the journey across the sea and was not only a signer of the Mayflower Compact but served as Governor of Plymouth 5 times over a 30-year period, is quoted as having said, *"Thus out of small beginnings greater things have been produced by His hand that made all things of nothing, and gives being to all things that are; and, as one small candle may light a thousand, so the light here kindled hath shone unto many..."* It would be courageous men and women like Bradford who would establish the church as the centerpiece of this new land.

When you look at the settlements in those original colonies, you would find the church literally at the very center of the town and their lives. For centuries churches would serve as the gathering place for "government" type meetings. Strangely, today we have gone from the church buildings as welcome places in which to govern a people to government buildings where the church is not welcome. The Ten Commandments are actually being removed in a growing number of places.

Let me be very clear. I am not saying that the government of our land, under the Constitution ever had the purpose and mission of the advancement of the gospel. That responsibility rests solely upon the church. The government is not supposed to interfere with the churches' purpose, though they are. Increasingly it is doing so through laws and judicial decisions. In fact, I am thankful that it is not the government's mission. When I see how poorly it has run everything else, the last thing I would desire is the government's endorsement, help or input.

What I am saying clearly is that the church must return to its clear mission in this world. That is to be a light. We must stop hiding under the bowl of indifference, apathy and lethargy. We should not be afraid to speak truth, in fact we need to speak the truth above the lies that have infiltrated our culture.

In the final chapter, we will discuss the need for the church to reengage in the culture, to be a change agent in our communities and to work together to return the "moral compass" and "values gyroscope" to the governing of our country. If we the church do not do so, this plane will meet terra firma, leaving a legacy of destruction and chaos for the next generation. But first, we will tackle another bible, and that's the bible of Progressives.

11

PLAYBOOKS, TRUTH
AND MORALITY

I want you to get a picture of this in your mind. It's the week before the final game of the season. It is a winner-takes-all scenario, with the crown, the ring and the title going to the victor of this game. You are sitting in the head coach's office. The walls are filled with various pictures of winning teams through the season. Interspersed are pictures of the team's superstars and most valuable players. There are numerous posters alongside with inspirational quotes on winning. To your left there is a large display case filled with trophies. To your right, a large portrait hangs encased in an elaborate frame that is spotlighted from above. It is the team's most winning coach of all time, a man who inspired many along the way. For now, you are focused on what is directly ahead of you: coaches attentive to what the head coach is saying.

It seems the entire coaching staff is dumbstruck about what to do in the upcoming game. The opponent is an enigma. Their coaching staff is not nearly as brilliant as those on your team. The talent of their players is eclipsed by the power and strength of your team. But for some odd reason it seems that every time the home team meets them on the field, the best laid plans of your team fall apart and you are left with defeat.

Your team's coaches have closely reviewed every game and scouted film of the opponent in action. You've studied former coaches and players to see if you can discover their secret of success. You have even gone so far as to compromise your own game goals and objectives in hopes of beating them at their own game—a philosophy of, "if you can't beat them join them."

However, today is going to be different. You see something in the coach's eyes that tell you today is indeed going to be a game changer. You begin to sense some hope rising in the room and you await with bated breath for the revelation of what will be different this time. Your anxious waiting is finally rewarded as the head coach pulls from his desk drawer a leather bound book, well-worn and tattered from use over many years. It is the opposing team's playbook. In between the aging front cover and back cover is every play the team has developed, complete with diagrams, principles and things learned in the years of actually running these plays. The understanding of the team's plans, objectives and schemes will allow you to get one step ahead of their plays and defeat them in the end. The Apostle Paul admonished the Corinthians to be cognizant of their opponent's methods and plans when he told them to be aware of Satan's schemes so that they would not be outwitted by him.[266]

Sue and I, along with countless others believe that today we stand on the precipice of such a time in our nation. We are in the final days which will determine whether or not our once-great nation will turn back to the principles it was founded upon and which made it great, or whether we will progress toward a repeated history of the also once-great Roman Empire, which fell not from an outside enemy, but from the enemy within. Sadly for me, watching our President swing his golf club in moments when he should be leading our country, is far too reminiscent of Nero's own fiddling. The good news is that while the game may be well into the final quarter, the game is not over. I believe we have the opportunity to learn from our opponent's tactics and bring about a game-changing strategy in the final minutes of the quarter.

The Progressive Movement, is much more than a political party or even a specific agenda, though both are necessary for the Progressives to achieve their goal. Their playbook is an open source of the philosophies and ideologies of their game. It is even referred to as the bible of Progressives. It is *Rules for Radicals* by Saul Alinsky. In this book, written shortly before Alinsky's death in 1973, he presents 12 rules for how to organize people to accomplish a chosen goal. These 12 rules can be summarized as follows:

- RULE 1: "Power is not only what you have, but what the enemy thinks you have." Power is derived from 2 main sources – money and people. "Have-Nots" must build power from flesh and blood.

- RULE 2: "Never go outside the expertise of your people." It results in confusion, fear and retreat. Feeling secure adds to the backbone of anyone.

- RULE 3: "Whenever possible, go outside the expertise of the enemy." Look for ways to increase insecurity, anxiety and uncertainty.

- RULE 4: "Make the enemy live up to its own book of rules." If the rule is that every letter gets a reply, send 30,000 letters. You can kill them with this because no one can possibly obey all of their own rules.

- RULE 5: "Ridicule is man's most potent weapon." There is no defense. It's irrational. It's infuriating. It also works as a key pressure point to force the enemy into concessions.

- RULE 6: "A good tactic is one your people enjoy." They'll keep doing it without urging and come back to do more. They're doing their thing, and will even suggest better ones.

- RULE 7: "A tactic that drags on too long becomes a drag." Don't become old news.

- RULE 8: "Keep the pressure on. Never let up." Keep trying new things to keep the opposition off balance. As the opposition masters one approach, hit them from the flank with something new.

• RULE 9: "The threat is usually more terrifying than the thing itself." Imagination and ego can dream up many more consequences than any activist.

• RULE 10: "If you push a negative hard enough, it will push through and become a positive." Violence from the other side can win the public to your side because the public sympathizes with the underdog.

• RULE 11: "The price of a successful attack is a constructive alternative." Never let the enemy score points because you're caught without a solution to the problem.

• RULE 12: "Pick the target, freeze it, personalize it, and polarize it." Cut off the support network and isolate the target from sympathy. Go after people and not institutions; people hurt faster than institutions.[267]

And Now This from Our Sponsor

Let's begin with knowing the author of this modern day playbook. Saul David Alinsky (January 30, 1909 – June 12, 1972) was an American community organizer and writer. He is generally considered to be the founder of modern community-organizing. He was born in Chicago, Illinois, in 1909 to Russian Jewish immigrant parents, the only surviving son of Benjamin Alinsky's marriage to his second wife, Sarah Tannenbaum Alinsky. Alinsky stated during an interview that his parents never became involved in the "new socialist movement." He added that they were "strict Orthodox, their whole life revolved around work and synagogue."[268]

Alinsky, as we have stated, is best known for authoring *Rules for Radicals,* which is the primer for community organizing. It is also the ideological blueprint for how to create a socialist movement while on the playing field of a capitalist home team. *Rules for Radicals* has had a profound impact upon today's leaders of the Progressive Movement, Hillary Clinton and Barack Obama. Newt Gingrich is quoted as saying that Obama draws his "understanding of America" from "Saul Alinsky, radical left-wingers, and people who don't like the classical America."[269] Hillary Clinton wrote a 92 page thesis while attending Wellesley College called "THERE IS ONLY THE FIGHT . . . An Analysis of the Alinsky Modol."[270] Clinton, Obama and other leaders of the Progressive Movement employ the tactics of *Rules for Radicals* as their playbook/bible because these strategies are effective especially when the opposition begins to leave a void of leadership and resolve. This is why the Progressive agenda is gaining ground— not so much from a winning formula, but due to a failing opponent which seems to have checked out momentarily.

Let's take a little closer look at *Rules for Radicals*. First of all, you can't get past the opening dedication page where Alinsky dedicates his work to none other than Lucifer. "Lest we forget at least an over the shoulder acknowledgement to the very first radical: from all our legends, mythology, and history...the first radical known to man who rebelled against the establishment and did it so effectively that he at least won his own kingdom---Lucifer."—Saul Alinsky.[271]

Then There's This from the Bible

With that kind of honor ceded to Satan, whom Alinksy considered the first among his kind, one cannot help but think an examination of an older playbook might be in order. Motivated by the first radical Alinsky, wrote what he called *A Pragmatic Primer for Realistic Radicals*. Saul Alinsky took almost 200 pages to write his playbook, but Satan (Lucifer) needs only one simple paragraph in God's play-book, the Holy Bible, to reveal his own radical strategy which hasn't changed for centuries. Let's examine the strategy he uses in the Garden of Eden.

Lucifer's chapter of *Rules for Radicals* begins here:

> Genesis 3:1-7 Now the serpent was more crafty than any of the wild animals the LORD God had made. He said to the woman, "Did God really say, 'You must not eat from any tree in the garden'?" The woman said to the serpent, "We may eat fruit from the trees in the garden, but God did say, 'You must not eat fruit from the tree that is in the middle of the garden, and you must not touch it, or you will die.'" "You will not surely die," the serpent said to the woman. "For God knows that when

you eat of it your eyes will be opened, and you will be like God, knowing good and evil." When the woman saw that the fruit of the tree was good for food and pleasing to the eye, and also desirable for gaining wisdom, she took some and ate it. She also gave some to her husband, who was with her, and he ate it. Then the eyes of both of them were opened, and they realized they were naked; so they sewed fig leaves together and made coverings for themselves.

God tells us that Satan is crafty, and not just a little crafty, but "more crafty." Merriam Webster's online dictionary defines "crafty" as being "adept in the use of subtlety and cunning." As shocking as it might appear, this accounts for the political correctness of our day. That's a warning that should bring us to our feet - or drive us to our knees - because our enemy knows how to sucker-punch us.

Now let's consider how his craftiness played out with Eve. He hit her with the one question that could plant a seed of confusion and a seed of doubt at the same time. When Satan asked, "Did God really say, 'You must not eat from any tree in the garden'?," it wasn't a question that would have confused Eve. In fact, she knew the answer immediately. What she didn't realize - so did Satan. He asked the one question that would cause Eve to let her defenses down and maybe even allow a little pride to build. She replied quickly:

> We may eat fruit from the trees in the garden but God did say, "You must not eat fruit from the tree that is in the middle of the garden, and you must not touch it, or you will die.

What Satan accomplished with one simple, seemingly-harmless question forever changed the world and man's relationship with His Creator. Satan questioned, and Eve, perhaps in an attempt to impress the Serpent, added to God's commandment something that God never said. God's instruction was simple --- do not eat. He never said do not touch, but Eve began her slippery slope by putting words into God's mouth that were contrary to his instruction.

Once Eve had believed her own lie, the serpent was ready for the knockout punch. The serpent said to Eve, "you will not surely die. For God knows that when you eat of it your eyes will be opened, and you will be like God, knowing good and evil." And there we have it. The first rule from the first radical: Sow the seed of temptation, doubt and a desire to possess that which is presently unknown. Create within Eve a sense that there is more to life than that which she has been given by The Creator. A contemporary approach is, if you don't have it and you want it, all you need to do is to name it and claim it.

As a result of this masterful deception, Eve responded:

> When the woman saw that the fruit of the tree was good for food and pleasing to the eye, and also desirable for gaining wisdom, she took some and ate it. She also gave some to her husband, who was with her, and he ate it. Then the eyes of both of them were opened, and they realized they were naked; so they sewed fig leaves together and made coverings for themselves.

Every temptation known to man is a lie wrapped in the subtlety of "look what you don't have." Saul Alinsky would see the world as divided between the "Haves" and the "Have-Nots." And he would begin his pragmatic primer on realistic radicals with Rule One – "Power is not only what you have, but what the enemy thinks you have." Power is derived from two main sources: money and people. "Have-Nots" must build power from flesh and blood."[272] He puts it this way: "In the world of give and take, tactics is the art of how to take and how to give. Here our concern is with the tactic of taking; how the Have-Nots can take away power from the Haves."[273]

The Haves, the Have-Nots and the Have-Somes

The entire Progressive Movement in America is built around Rule One and the premise of Haves and Have-Nots. It wraps itself in the subtlety of helping the poor, the oppressed and the disenfranchised when at its heart it is a strategy to destroy the Haves until only one class remains under a powerful all-encompassing government. Surprisingly, one of the major threats to their plan is the middle class. This is why the middle class (I guess we can call them the Have-Somes) is the most endangered species in America. The Have-Somes are the producers in our nation. They keep the Haves – having, and they give hope to the Have-Nots that there is a better solution than the Nanny Culture currently being propagated by our government. The middle class stands in the pathway of the socialist revolution of which the acolytes of Alinsky have dreamed. In the Alinsky utopia, the producers in the nation are ridiculed and minimized while those who drink the Kool-Aid offered by bureaucrats and those who consume others wealth are heralded, empowered and then invited to consume even more.

At least for now, most of the Haves still have. They have fared well under the initial takeover by Progressives. Despite the economic turndown, they have held on to their 1% status. The smart ones realize that once the middle class is destroyed, they too will be destroyed in very short order, for without a strong middle class the Haves will HAVE to foot the bill for the Progressives' new world order. If you somehow think that working for evil corporations like Wal-Mart is bad, just wait until the whole society works for the government. The government then becomes the only Haves who possess anything. One should consider the track record of the government and how they run things. Can you say IRS?

Among the Haves, there are those who loudly and proudly sound the battle cry of the Progressives and, like lemmings, are leading others to walk over the edge. They are called the Hollywood elite, and the reality of tinsel town and the kind of fantasy world in which they have grown, with the exception of the few who, like the middle class, are ridiculed and minimized, will never get it simply because they are not producers, but consumers of others' wealth. They love to rail against corporate bigwigs who take home fat checks while paying their employees moderate to low wages. Yet they themselves take home more from one movie than a CEO makes in a year. How much of their income do you think they want to share with the person in the lobby taking the ticket stubs? Their clamor is blatant hypocrisy!

Something else stands clearly in the way of the Progressives' agenda. It is more powerful than the middle class, more powerful than invading armies, more powerful than a speeding bullet. Truth is the greatest challenge faced by today's radicals because truth will always triumph in the end. Truth is a very scary thing to Progressives because people are set free by truth. Jesus said you will know the truth and the truth will set you free. This is why the real battle line is centered upon the battle for truth and the hearts and the minds of our nation. The biggest causality of the Progressive assault has been truth. Alinsky calls for a total disregard for truth among his followers. He puts it this way. "An organizer (Progressive) working in and for an open society (socialist society) is in an ideological dilemma."[274] To begin with, he does not have a fixed truth - truth to him is relative and changing; everything to him was relative and changing.

In what Alinsky calls "the fourth rule of the ethics of means and ends," he cites that "...judgment must be made in the context of the times in which the action occurred and not from any other chronological vantage point."[275] In other words, there is no such thing as absolute truth or timeless principles by which we cannot reinterpret them to suit the ends we want to achieve. Both the Constitution and the Bible have been casualties of this scheme to throw the baby out with the bathwater. He goes on to say, "Moral rationalization is indispensable at ALL TIMES of action whether to justify the selection or the use of ends and means."[276]

We have been dealing with a culture of relativism and now have the first full generation of young people who have had only a steady diet of relativism. It permeates our country, this idea that truth is whatever I think truth is. I am my own author of truth. Sue has provided example after example of this in the first nine chapters of this book. I won't try to cover the ground again except to share my first encounter with relativism. In 1993, while serving as Youth Pastor at our church, the local cable company opted to start carrying the Playboy Channel and another adult-only channel. The signals were scrambled, but one could generally make out the images and the audio was very clear. I began to hear guys in my group talking about this and how they saw one thing or another through the scramble. To them it was funny. To me it was heartbreaking. I had struggled with an addiction to pornography which started when I was 11 years old. I knew too well the shame, the guilt, and the horrific image of women that it caused in me. I wanted badly to protect the youth I was pastoring. So, I made an appointment with the management of the cable company and appealed to them for a solution that would prevent at least the vulnerable eyes, hearts and minds of young people from being infected with a potentially lifelong struggle like the one I had faced. The management flatly refused any consideration of my request with this statement: "What is wrong for you may not be wrong for me. And what is right for me may not be right for you. Everybody decides what is right and wrong for themselves and therefore you have no place to tell me what is wrong or even to tell your students what is wrong." I was baffled by their response. My chin dropped to my chest as I observed their insensitivity and heard their refusal to consider a reasonable alternative. I asked the manager if what he was saying meant that if I thought that it was right for me to go get a gun, bring it in, aim it at his head and pull the trigger, would that make it right" His answer was unbelievably, "Yes for you that would be right." I could see clearly then that relative truth had arrived and was now taking away the hearts, the minds and the morals of people. The lack of a truth compass or gyroscope as we have said, leads only to chaos and anarchy. This is the tool of the radicals and the Progressive Movement.

The third and final blockade for this movement lies in the remnant of strong leadership in our nation that still "get it." Many of these leaders have not yet revealed themselves: Some are still developing, and some God is still appointing. However, make no mistake that a remnant of the faithful remain. In part we are discouraged, disappointed and disillusioned, but we are not defeated. I believe and am hopeful that we will see more appointed and anointed leaders stand up, speak out and prayerfully-but-forcefully turn this nation back to its Founders' principles. It can't come too soon for Sue and me.

Alinsky's final rule - number 12 - is his retaliation on any frontal assault from a strong and patriotic conservative person. "Pick the target, freeze it, personalize it, and polarize it." He goes on to say:

> In conflict tactics there are certain rules that the organizer should always regard as universalities. One is that the opposition must be singled out as the target and 'frozen.'... There is a constant, and somewhat legitimate passing of the buck...the same evasion of responsibility is to be found in all areas of life...[277]

It seems that President Harry Truman's sign from his desk in the oval office that read, "The buck stops here," was replaced by President Obama with a sign that says, "The buck passes by here too fast for anyone to even see."

Progressives love to shift the blame. Six years have passed and every problem is still blamed on President George W. Bush. The scandals that plague our current administration are blamed on anyone but the current administration. This requires choosing a target, freezing it, personalizing it and polarizing it. Rule number 5 states this even more clearly, "Ridicule is man's most potent weapon." In the garden, Satan trapped Eve with the same strategy: "For God knows that when you eat of it your eyes will be opened, and you will be like God, knowing good and evil." From the time Lucifer was cast from heaven, God became the target to freeze and polarize. It's the oldest trick in the book. This represents the deception of Lucifer from eternity-past to the present time. Isaiah 14:12-16 tells of Lucifer's desire to supplant God. (Alinsky's admiration for Satan's schemes fit like a hand in a glove.) In describing a situation in which he had been involved during his days in Chicago, Alinsky stated that it was time to start "…an intensive campaign of ridicule, insults and taunting defiance…."[278] Have we not watched this scenario play out again and again from Progressives at any point where it might appear that their opposition is gaining ground? They already have the hearts of much of the mass media in this country, and they count on the media to win the hearts of the public for their cause. Fortunately, while they are succeeding to some degree, the remnant remains.

What Shapes Us is Important

That which shapes a man's character, his philosophies and his actions gives us a deeper insight into who he is, where he has been and where he is going. In an article written by John Fund and published in National Review titled "Still the Alinsky Playbook," Fund asks the question, "Where did Alinsky get this amorality?" He wrote:

> Clues can be found in a Playboy magazine interview he gave in 1972, just before his death. In the closest thing to a memoir Alinsky left, he told how he decided to do his (never-completed) doctoral dissertation in the 1930s on the Al Capone mob, and to do it as "an inside job." He caught the eye of Big Ed Stash, the mob's top executioner, and convinced him he could be trusted as a sort of mob mascot who would interpret its methods to the outside world. "He introduced me to Frank Nitti, known as the Enforcer, Capone's number-two man," Alinsky told Playboy. "Nitti took me under his wing. I called him the Professor and I became his student. Nitti's boys took me everywhere."

Alinsky recalled that he "learned a hell of a lot about the uses and abuses of power from the mob," and that he applied that knowledge "later on, when I was organizing." The Playboy interviewer asked, "Didn't you have any compunction about consorting with — if not actually assisting — murderers?" Alinsky replied: "None at all, since there was nothing I could do to stop them from murdering. . . . I was a nonparticipating observer in their professional activities, although I joined their social life of food, drink, and women. Boy, I sure participated in that side of things — it was heaven."

Unlike the mob members he hung out with, Alinsky never coveted great wealth. "He was essentially a thrill-seeker who admitted he was easily bored and always had to stir things up," says Lee Stranahan, who was a blogger for the Huffington Post until last year, when his research into Alinsky-inspired groups soured him on the Left. "His followers are even more ideological and relentless than he was."[279]

"Any means to reaching our end" is the mantra of this movement. Today's Alinsky devotees are much more determined, much more powerful, better funded and better positioned than Alinsky himself ever dreamed.

Why this is Vital to our Future

At best, I have only been able to give a brief, but hopefully insightful, peek into *Rules for Radicals* and the playbook Progressives are following with reckless abandon. Sue has suggested that perhaps I preach on each of Alinsky's 12 rules from a Biblical perspective. Perhaps I will do that and share those with you in the future. For now, I give you these things to consider in hope that you will awaken to what is happening in our country. Too many are still scratching their heads and asking, "Who switched the price tags?" It is not difficult to discover that this is not "just happening." Make no mistake that this movement has been progressing forward for many decades and now, especially in these last six years, it is emboldened and overt. Critical people are in place in high positions, and they are one step closer to the socialist takeover they envision. This is an appeal to ask you to stop listening to what they are saying and to start watching what they are doing. We have written this with a belief that America's greatest days lie ahead, but we must first learn the lessons from our past and from our present, and we must engage like never before in an activism of our own. Before we move on to some final, but important, thoughts about our future ahead as a nation, let me leave you with the words of a 20th century leader who understood what he called "the shining city on a hill."

"You and I have a rendezvous with destiny.

We will preserve for our children this, the last best hope of man on earth,

or we will sentence them to take the first step into a thousand years of darkness.

If we fail, at least let our children and our children's children

say of us we justified our brief moment here.

We did all that could be done."

Ronald Reagan[280]

12

SPIRITUAL REVIVAL AND AMERICAN RENEWAL

"A man injured on the job filed an insurance claim. The insurance company requested more information, so the man wrote the insurance company the following letter of explanation:

Dear Sirs:

I am writing in response to your request concerning clarification of the information I supplied in block #11 on the insurance form, which asked for the cause of the injury. I answered, "Trying to do the job alone." I trust that the following explanation will be sufficient.

I am a bricklayer by trade. On the date of the injury, I was working alone, laying brick around the top of a three-story building. When I finished the job, I had about five hundred pounds of brick left over. Rather than carry the bricks down by hand, I decided to put them into a barrel and lower them by a pulley that was fastened to the top of the building.

I secured the end of the rope at ground level, went back up to the top of the building, loaded the bricks into the barrel, and pushed it over the side. I then went back down to the ground and untied the rope, holding it securely to insure the slow descent of the barrel. As you will note in block #6 of the insurance form, I weigh 145 pounds. At the shock of being jerked off the ground so swiftly by the five hundred pounds of bricks in the barrel, I lost my presence of mind and forgot to let go of the rope.

Between the second and third floors I met the barrel. This accounts for the bruises and lacerations on my upper body. Fortunately, I retained enough presence of mind to maintain my tight hold on the rope and proceeded rapidly up the side of the building, not stopping until my right hand was jammed in the pulley. This accounts for my broken thumb (see block #4). Despite the pain, I continued to hold tightly to the rope. Unfortunately, at approximately the same time, the barrel hit the ground and the bottom fell out of the barrel. Devoid of the weight of the bricks, the barrel now weighed about fifty pounds. I again refer you to block #6, where my weight is listed. I began a rapid descent.

In the vicinity of the second floor, I met the barrel coming up. This explains the injury to my legs and lower body. Slowed only slightly, I continued my descent, landing on the pile of bricks. Fortunately, my back was only sprained. I am sorry to report, however, that at this point I again lost my presence of mind—and let go of the rope.

I trust that this answers your concern. Please note that I am finished trying to do the job alone."[281]

There was a long and arduous process that led to the settling and eventual founding of America the Beautiful. A group of English men, women and children who believed in the purity and inerrancy of the Bible were ridiculed and ostracized by the British state church. These believers were united in their unwavering faith in God's Word and saw this situation as a spiritual, cultural and political problem. They sought God, they heard from God and they obeyed God. Their obedience was so radical that today we see very little example of that kind of radical faith in God. For the Pilgrims, as we know them today. Finding another European country or even relocating to the "New World" was all about

God. It was a dream from God, for God and through God. Today, we have become almost independent of God. It is as if a new declaration of independence has been written, this time declaring self as the only dependable source of life, liberty and the pursuit of happiness. We are trying to live our life without God as the source of life.

So Who's to Blame?

By this point, one might make an assumption that Sue and I are blaming the Progressive Movement, liberal ideology and even Satan himself for the woes of America. To the contrary, we are merely pointing out the worldview and mission of those movements and how it is shaking the foundations of our beloved country. Irish political philosopher Edmund Burke is often credited for having said:

> The only thing necessary for the triumph of evil is for good men to do nothing."[282] He also is quoted as saying, "It is not enough in a situation of trust in the commonwealth, that a man means well to his country; it is not enough that in his single person he never did an evil act, but always voted according to his conscience, and even harangued against every design which he apprehended to be prejudicial to the interests of his country.[283]

What a sound warning these words should be to our ears during these days. However, Edmund Burke was not first to sound this warning. God first declared this warning nearly 3,000 years ago to Cain, the son of Adam and Eve. But on Cain and his offering he did not look with favor. So Cain was very angry, and his face was downcast. Then the LORD said to Cain, "Why are you angry? Why is your face downcast? If you do what is right, will you not be accepted? **But if you do not do what is right, sin is crouching at your door;** it desires to have you, but you must master it." (Genesis 4:5-7)

No, I do not blame the Progressive Movement for our country's slippery slope. I place, and I believe God places, the blame on His church. God said, "Blessed is the nation whose God is the LORD, the people he chose for his inheritance." (Psalm 33:12) The Apostle Peter wrote to us, "If you suffer, it should not be as a murderer or thief or any other kind of criminal, or even as a meddler.

However, if you suffer as a Christian, do not be ashamed, but praise God that you bear that name. **For it is time for judgment to begin with the family of God…"** (1 Peter 4:15-17)

Increasingly through the centuries, the church has abdicated its God-given purpose and mission thereby creating a void in which evil may prevail. In the last century, we have sought to be professional. We have hired professionals and we have created professional structures and organizations. We build professional-style meeting centers. We offer professional programs. The church is more professional today than ever before, yet, in the quest toward professionalism, we have lost purposefulness. The void this is leaving is devastating to the people of our nation. Those of us who claim to follow Christ will stand before an Almighty God one day and give an account. It won't matter if we were a pastor, a deacon, a church leader, a Sunday School teacher or just a pew warmer. We will give an account to God for the stewardship of our lives, our possessions, our time and the talents that God has invested in us and through us. We won't be given a pass simply because we felt like there really wasn't anything that we could do to change the hearts and minds of this nation. While we point our finger back at the Progressive Movement or that pastor who didn't do his job, God's finger will be pointed right at us.

If you "attend" church, I want you to know that you can't really do that. Nobody ever "attends" church. Oh, you can take up a space in a building with others. You can sing songs, carry your Bible, pray and even drop some coins into the offering plate, but you cannot "attend" church. You can only "BE" the church. The church isn't the building, the programs, the professionals or even the "doers" in the gathering. The church is the present, living, breathing, life-hanging-Body of Christ left upon this earth to do good, so that no void exists for evil to gain a stronghold. I am not naïve enough to think that all evil would be eradicated if the church would just be the church. That will not happen until the final hour when Christ returns. We are not just seeing the presence of evil around us. We are sliding ever closer to strongholds of evil because we, the church, are hiding behind our four walls trying, for the most part, to stay as comfortable through the storm as we can. A stronghold occurs when the prevailing attitude is the acceptance of what God calls evil.

Our early settlers clearly understood the requirement of absolute values to guard and guide the people. The Founders clearly sought a guarding and guiding from God for the establishment of the laws of this land. They knew this would be the only way to keep order amidst the growing diversity of our nation, and so they would turn repeatedly to the God of order. Look at creation and see the intricate design and order that science affirms is there. Look at our human bodies, fearfully and wonderfully made, and see the complexity of its established order. Then consider what happens when we don't care for God's creation and we destroy it with human pollutants. Consider what happens to the body when it is not cared for properly and sickness and disease enter. There is also an established order for marriage. But what happens when we allow others to redefine it and then celebrate their own new design that has no order? The family has an order and design. Sex was given a design and order, but we have allowed a casting-off of that design and order and now the nation is bound under a sexual stronghold that prevails in almost every avenue of life. Through His Word, God has given us the established order for all of life. He has established order for businesses and corporations and order for government. Most of all, God established order for our individual lives. When we seek to serve our own selfish good, and not the good of God's order and glory, we have left a void in our own lives in which evil will prevail.

Where Did We Get Off Track?

Chuck Colson, founder of Prison Fellowship Ministries, an international outreach to prisons, was converted to Christianity before being indicted on Watergate-related charges in the 1970s (Google Watergate). He became one of the strongest and most influential voices calling the church and Christians back to being agents of change in the culture in which God placed them. In 2007, Colson helped write an article for *Christianity Today* that was subtitled "We're on the verge of destroying a key pillar of civilization." In the article, he shares an episode that took place in a Christian club in a middle school.

A graduate of our Centurion program (an intensive course in biblical worldview) sponsors a voluntary Christian club at her local middle school. Forty-three students eagerly signed up for the 13-week course.

Everything went well until the students reached lesson 10, which led them through a series of choices to learn the difference between matters of taste and truth. One of the choices, "believing Islam, Buddhism, or Christianity" flashed on the screen.

Our Centurion—I'll call her Joanne—told me "the students went nuts." She was shocked when seven of the eight small-group leaders, supposedly mature Christians, balked at distinguishing Christianity as true and other religions as false.

Joanne urged them to talk to their parents or pastors, believing these authority figures would straighten them out. The next day, they came back with their answers—and they were appalling. One teen's pastor said that no one can be sure of truth, that "it's all perspective." Parents of the seven leaders agreed that their teens shouldn't say that Christianity alone is true, because that could offend others. One girl had written a paper on "Why We Shouldn't Hurt Others' Feelings by Claiming Our Way Is Right." Joanne was forced to shelve chapter 10. "They can't teach what they don't believe," she said.

If this is representative of what's going on in the church, we've got problems. We should be concerned not just about discipleship, but also about whether we are losing what sociologist Robert Bellah calls our "community of memory.[284]

Along our journey, we have discussed how relativism and relative truth has crept into our culture through many avenues where Progressives have great influence, from Hollywood, to the news media and sadly, to public schools. Their influence is based on the claim that "all truth is relative." But once again, I don't assign the responsibility for these matters on the venues I have mentioned. Rather, I make that assignment on the house of God. The church, I believe, has allowed the spread of this infection by straying from the truth of Scripture. Frankly, we have become so accustomed to the culture, and so in love with the culture, that our own version of "American Idol" plays out in our sanctuaries week after week. And who is that idol? Why it's us. We have made ourselves the center of attention. This has been the pathway for relativism to enter the church. I choose my version of the truth, and if I am as tolerant as the world expects me to be, then at the same time I must accept your version of the truth, even if the two truths are polar opposites.

As a church leader myself, I have noticed the growing trend over the last four decades of people who seem to ask more and more of the church. Jesus said that He came to serve, not to be served, but most pastors I speak to estimate that easily 80% of their attendees "came to be served, not to serve."[285] People expect the church to provide them comfort - spiritually, emotionally and physically. Our church facilities need to be modern, slick and attractive. We should learn to control the temperature and the volume of music at a level with which everyone is comfortable. We come to church and do not expect to be offended in any way, shape or form. The church needs to have tight control on rowdy children, noisy teenagers, how much the pastor is paid and the proper use of his time in accordance with our expectations. Convenient parking and large comfortable seating are a top priority for the church in which God would lead us to worship. Billy Graham said:

> Many churches of all persuasions are hiring research agencies to poll neighborhoods, asking what kind of church they prefer. Then the local churches design themselves to fit the desires of the people. True faith in God that demands selflessness is being replaced by trendy religion that serves the selfish.[286]

And while our previously stated statistics on pastors show clearly the frightening number of them that are burned out, or approaching burnout, it seems that church leadership has responded to all of these growing expectations upon the resources of the church by expecting less and less from the people. When a people who expect more from the church and a church that expects less from the people are combined, it has become a civic organization that gets people together for the purpose of doing some good things. Yes, our churches are known for good things, but are they known for God things? Is the church changing the culture, as it has done for centuries, or is the culture changing the church? What the Pilgrims involved themselves in was not a political solution to the cultural ills of the day, but a spiritual solution. United by faith, they sought to let God guide their steps into a new world, and so He did. May I suggest that we need a revival of radical obedience to God-birthed Spiritual solutions again today in the church?

In 2012, Billy Graham wrote this:

> Some years ago, my wife, Ruth, was reading the draft of a book I was writing. When she finished a section describing the terrible downward spiral of our nation's moral standards and the idolatry of worshiping false gods such as technology and sex, she startled me by exclaiming, "If God doesn't punish America, He'll have to apologize to Sodom and Gomorrah."
>
> She was probably thinking of a passage in Ezekiel where God tells why He brought those cities to ruin. "Now this was the sin of ... Sodom: She and her daughters were arrogant, overfed and unconcerned; they did not help the poor and needy. They were haughty and did detestable things before me. Therefore I did away with them as you have seen" (Ezekiel 16:49–50, NIV).
>
> I wonder what Ruth would think of America if she were alive today. In the years since she made that remark, millions of babies have been aborted and our nation seems largely unconcerned. Self-centered indulgence, pride, and a lack of shame over sin are now emblems of the American lifestyle.
>
> Just a few weeks ago in a prominent city in the South, Christian chaplains who serve the police department were ordered to no longer mention the Name of Jesus in prayer. It was reported that during a recent police-sponsored event, the only person allowed to pray was someone who addressed "the being in the room." Similar scenarios are now commonplace in towns across America. Our society strives to avoid any possibility of offending anyone—except God.
>
> Yet the farther we get from God, the more the world spirals out of control.
>
> My heart aches for America and its deceived people. The wonderful news is that our Lord is a God of mercy, and He responds to repentance. In Jonah's day, Nineveh was the lone world superpower—wealthy,

unconcerned, and self-centered. When the Prophet Jonah finally traveled to Nineveh and proclaimed God's warning, people heard and repented.[287]

Not Just Possible...Not Just Probable...But Promised!

A decade ago, I experienced something that I had anticipated since I first moved to the state of Florida in 1980. Many years would come and go with reports of the possibility of a hurricane hitting our area. Watches and warnings would come and go year after year, but no hurricane. Finally, in 2004, our town was hit by not one, but two hurricanes, one right after the other. The destruction was heavy and the days of recovery were tough, but two things stand out in my mind as powerful events caused by the hurricanes. The first effect was, it seemed that no matter where you went in town, every single fence that separated properties was blown down and destroyed. The second effect that was noticeable was that the "fences" between the people and churches were blown down as well. Churches came together and worked together for the common good. Our denominational, ethnic and geographical boundaries could not hold us back in the midst of the devastation around us and the recovery that needed to happen.

For weeks I spent most of my time taking crews from our church around to tarp roofs and cut up fallen trees. After the work was done I would sit and have a glass of tea with someone I was now bound to only because we owned some chain saws and had loaded up on tarps before the winds came. In fact, I spent much more time in those days doing hurricane recovery than I did in trying to prepare a sermon. At the time, our church met in three small modular buildings - basically larger mobile homes. While one would expect total destruction of this type of structure in high winds, they survived with no damage. However, other churches did not fare as well. As a result, we welcomed three other churches to share our modest little buildings until theirs could be repaired or replaced. We hosted a Hispanic congregation, an African American congregation and a Pentecostal congregation. Ten years later, the Hispanic church family remains with us. I will never forget that first Christmas after the hurricanes. The four churches held a Christmas Eve service together. The unity that was evident in that room that night still rings in my heart as an actual taste of heaven.

Sadly, the neighborhoods began to build their fences back around their houses, and the people and the churches began to build their own fences back as well, believing that our worst threat would be another hurricane. Yet what has been described in this book holds far more potential for damage to this generation and the ones to come. We must awaken spiritually once again in our church houses and our government houses to the reality of Rome's burning while Nero fiddles.

Like Billy Graham, I believe there is hope for America. Like many others in our nation today, I am praying for a revival that brings American renewal. Former President Ronald Reagan once said,

> I believe with all my heart that standing up for America means standing up for the God who has so blessed our land. We need God's help to guide our nation through stormy seas. But we can't expect Him to protect America in a crisis if we just leave Him over on the shelf in our day-to-day living."[288]

So I call upon you who claim to believe in God to seek Him with all of your heart, to hear Him speak and to obey with reckless abandon, serving God and serving others. I call upon you to stand for truth, not as you want it to be, but as it is from God's Holy Word. I think that revival is not just possible and not even just probable. I believe it is promised when united by faith we join together in the following pursuits.

Pray Boldly

The following Bible verse is often quoted as a key to revival:"…if my people, who are called by my name, will humble themselves and pray and seek my face and turn from their wicked ways, then will I hear from heaven and will forgive their sin and will heal their land." 2 Chronicles 7:14 (NIV) If you ask most Christians will say they want revival, but the reality is we want revival without having to humble ourselves - as it might wound our precious pride - and especially without having to turn from our wicked ways. By wicked ways, I am not just speaking of the addict and the prostitute, I am also speaking of the one who turns his back to a neighbor's need...the one who refuses to forgive those who have hurt him, the one who quickly tries to pluck the splinter from another's eye while a lumber yard exists in his own. Stop asking what it will take for revival to come to America or even to your own church. Ask instead, what it will take for revival to come to your heart. If enough of us do that, hear God and then obey, nationwide revival is on its way.

Live Holy

God knows we do not and probably will not live perfect lives. But He has called us to be holy: ...for it is written: "Be holy, because I am holy." 1 Peter 1:16 (NIV) God has called us to live holy, markedly separate lives; i.e. a life that looks like God more than it looks like the culture. This call is not just for the way we dress or the words we use. It arises from the deepest part of our hearts because the real us will ultimately be seen by those around us.

Serve Selflessly

When I consider the nature of a servant that Jesus became and how He Himself called us to love and serve one another, I can't help but be mindful that Jesus said to do this even for our enemies. "But love your enemies, do good to them, and lend to them without expecting to get anything back. Then your reward will be great, and you will be sons of the Most High, because he is kind to the ungrateful and wicked." **Luke 6:35 (NIV)** When we are seen to be a loving, serving and generous people, the world will want to know what makes us different.

Engage Culture Graciously

As Christians, we are not called to isolate ourselves from the world but to insulate ourselves from the temptations of the world. While I believe we have a

civic privilege and duty to participate in our governmental process by supporting candidates, voting and even running for office if led by God, the real change
our nation is desperate for can only come from a spiritual awakening. You have
been placed on earth as witness to God's love and His purpose for humanity. It's
not your pastor's job or the deacon's or the church leaders'. It is a call upon all of
us who call upon God. For there is no difference between Jew and Gentile--the
same Lord is Lord of all and richly blesses all who call on him. "Everyone who
calls on the name of the Lord will be saved." How, then, can they call on the One
they have not believed in? And how can they believe in the One of whom they
have not heard? And how can they hear without someone preaching to them?
And how can they preach unless they are sent? As it is written, "How beautiful
are the feet of those who bring good news!" **Romans 10:12-15 (NIV)** Here's a
fundamental truth with which we must agree: While we are a nation of laws, and
laws serve a common good for the most part, legislation can only control morality to a degree. Legislation will never change morality. As Christians we must
work toward changed hearts that lead to changed lives.

Stand Firmly in Faith

I believe that in the days ahead we will see more and more attempts by our
government and by various other groups, to push the truth of the gospel deeper
and deeper into the closet. We must resist these attempts and meet them head on
with a strong faith and that refuses to back down. Of course, we can do this lovingly or we can do it offensively. May I suggest the former better serves the latter
every time and is more evident of the winsomeness of Christ? But stand we must.

What Race are You Running?

Greyhound racing, a popular betting sport in some parts of the
country, attracts crowds who enjoy watching incredibly sleek and beautiful dogs run as fast as they can around a track. Unlike racehorses, greyhounds run without the assistance of a jockey. To keep the dogs running
in the right direction, they are trained to chase a mechanical rabbit made

of fur as it zips along the track in front of them. A man in the press box electronically controls the speed of the rabbit, keeping the rabbit just out in front of the dogs. The dogs never catch up to it.

At a Florida track some years back, a big race was about to begin. The dogs crouched in their cages, ready to go, while betting spectators finished placing their wagers. At the proper moment, the gun went off. The man in the press box pushed his lever, starting the rabbit down the first stretch, while the cage doors flew open, releasing the dogs to take off after the little rabbit. As the rabbit made the first turn, however, an electrical short in the system caused the rabbit to come to a complete stop, to explode, and to go up in flames. Poof! All that was left was a bit of black stuff hanging on the end of a wire.

Their rabbit gone, the bewildered dogs didn't know how to act. According to news reports, several dogs simply stopped running and laid down on the track, their tongues hanging out. Two dogs, still frenzied with the chase, ran into a wall, breaking several ribs. Another dog began chasing his tail, while the rest howled at the people in the stands.[289]

Like racing greyhounds, we tend to pursue our chosen rabbit. We need some reason for living - for running the race. What is your goal, your purpose in life, your hope? What if it was taken away? Sadly, many people chase an illusion, a mechanical rabbit of sorts, which ultimately turns out to offer no hope at all. Perhaps, as you look at our nation today, that describes how you are feeling. Yes, America seems to be in a downward spiral, and we appear beyond hope. We can give up, give in or give ourselves to God.

Paul wrote that which kept him motivated to run the race: "For to me, to live is Christ" (Philippians 1:21). Jesus is the only one who can give us lasting purpose, meaning, and hope. Paul later wrote, "I press on toward the goal to win the prize for which God has called me heavenward in Christ Jesus." (Philippians 3:14)

To know Christ is the only lasting, eternal goal.

EPILOGUE

Roger and I have love of God and love of country in common. Another thing we have in common is we were both brought up in traditional Christian homes by parents who lived out Judeo-Christian values and tried their best to pass their worldview along to their children. The core values drilled into Roger and me at home and at Sunday school or Church remain with us today. The Judeo-Christian worldview is built on Truth. Not relative it's all about me truth, instead Christianity builds on the Truth Jesus spoke. Many parents today are too busy or do not wish to teach their children the Biblical worldview. A firm foundation is no longer being built for our children to stand upon.

The kind of character we speak of stands up for Truth no matter the cost.

After being met with protests and losing her bakery over her refusal to bake a cake for a lesbian couple, Melissa Klein took to social media to vent her frustrations:

Sweet Cakes by Melissa

Our culture has accepted 2 huge lies. The first is that if you disagree with someone's lifestyle, you must fear or hate them. Second is that to love someone means that you must agree with everything they believe or do. Both are nonsense. You don't have to compromise convictions to be compassionate.[290]

I quoted Dinesh D'Souza in this book because of my profound respect for his intellect and worldview. Our Judicial System holds a polar worldview.

"D'Souza to be Sent to Re-education Camp

By Richard Butrick

It seems that Dinesh D'Souza's problem is that his mindset is not up to date. He believes in such antiquarian notions as freedom of speech and worst of all he admires the U.S. Founding Fathers. The man is obviously sick and in need of "therapeutic counseling." This according Judge Richard M. Berman of Federal District Court in Manhattan who sentenced D'Souza, the conservative author and filmmaker of documentaries highly critical of President Obama. He was sentenced to five years probation and eight months in a "community confinement center" where he would be required to "undergo" therapeutic counseling. As the judge noted, D'Souza "just doesn't get it." And this therapeutic counseling? About campaign fraud? Methinks not. D'Souza is fully cognizant that he violated the law and faults himself and admits he rightfully must receive appropriate punishment. The counseling is for his antediluvian mindset.

Undergo?

Translation: he is to be PCd, multicultured, homophiled, and Zinned. The last being probably the most important. He is to be made to understand that it is U.S. imperialism, racism and sexism, nationalism, supremacism, and jingoism that is responsible for the mess the world is in now. This is especially true in the Mideast where justifiable Arab rage is wreaking havoc. It is a case of chickens coming home to roost. Moreover, he is to be made to realize that the real U.S. Founding Fathers are Saul Alinsky, Jeremiah Wright, and Jane Fonda. In short, he is to be made to see that being an American is nothing to be proud of.

> Theodore Dalrymple, one of the truly great essayists of our time, was quick to pick up on the Orwellian thought-control implications of "therapeutic counseling" for those who are critical of their government. He notes that, "The Soviets thought that dissent was crime and crime was disease: therefore, with them, dissent was disease." Are we there yet?[291]

Are we there yet?

Thank you for reading our book and God Bless.

(ENDNOTES)

1   http://www.brainyquote.com

2   http://www.merriam-webster.com/dictionary/laissez-faire

3   D'Souza, Dinesh, *America: Imagine A World Without Her*, Washington, D.C., Regnery Publishing, 2014. Pg. 223

4   http://www.prisonplanet.com/texas-public-school-curriculum-teaches-students-to-design-a-socialist-flag-and-that-christianity-is-a-cult.html

5   D'Souza 19.

6   D'Souza, Dinesh, *America: Imagine A World Without Her*, Washington, D.C., Regnery Publishing, 2014. Pg. 22.

7   http://en.wikipedia.org/wiki/Christopher_Columbus

8   D'Souza, Dinesh, *America: Imagine A World Without Her*, Washington, D.C., Regnery Publishing, 2014. Pg. 93.

9   http://www.mysecondthoughts.com/?p=1

10   Brad, Bright, *God is the Issue –Recapturing the Cultural Initiative*, Peachtree City, Georgia, New Life Publications, 2003, Pg. 24.

11   Limbaugh, David, *Persecution: How Liberals are Waging a War on Christianity*, New York: Regnery Publishing, 2003. Pg. 347.

12 http://www.original-republican.com/benjamin-franklin-on-public-service/

13 Skousen, W. Cleon, The 5000 Year Leap, The National Center for Constitutional Studies, 1981. Pg. 19.

14 Skousen 23.

15 http://www.biblicalchristianworldview.net/documents/quotesRonal-dReagan.pdf

16 http://www.ushistory.org/us/10f.asp

17 "Congress shall make no law respecting an establishment of religion, or prohibiting the free exercise thereof; or abridging the freedom of speech, or of the press; or the right of the people peaceably to assemble, and to petition the Government for a redress of grievances." http://www.constitution.org/billofr_.htm

18 D'Souza 46/47.

19 http://www.archives.gov/exhibits/charters/declaration_transcript.htm

20 D'Souza 41.

21 Colson, Charles, The Sky is Not Falling; Living Fearlessly in These Turbulent Times, Brentwood, Tennessee, Worthy Publishing, 2011, Pg. 29.

22 http://dictionary.reference.com/browse/bureaucrats

23 Skousen 116

24   Limbaugh, David, *Persecution: How Liberals are Waging a War on Christianity*, New York: Regnery Publishing, 2003. Pg. 350.

25   Colson, Charles, *The Sky is Not Falling; Living Fearlessly in These Turbulent Times*, Brentwood, Tennessee, Worthy Publishing, 2011, Pg. 133.

26   D'Souza 50.

27   Skousen 208.

28   http://www.washingtonpost.com/opinions/george-f-will-stopping-a-lawless-president/2014/06/20/377c4d6e-f7e5-11e3-a3a5-42be35962a52_story.html

29   Colson, Charles, *God & Government*, Grand Rapids, Michigan Zondervan, 2007, Pg. 271.

30   Colson, Charles, *God & Government*, Grand Rapids, Michigan Zondervan, 2007, Pg. 273.

31   http://ushistory.org/us/19c.asp

32   http://www.netplaces.com/american-government/the-vice-presidency/the-early-years.htm

33   Colson, Charles, The Sky is Not Falling; Living Fearlessly in These Turbulent Times, Brentwood, Tennessee, Worthy Publishing, 2011, Pg. 213-214.

34   http://conservative-daily.com/2013/11/12/holder-international-law-trumps-the-constitution/

35   Alinsky, Saul D., *Reveille for Radicals*, New York, Random House, 1946. Pg. 15.

36   D'Souza 77.

37   http://www.nbcnews.com/id/17388372/ns/politics-decision_08/t/
reading-hillary-rodhams-hidden-thesis/#.U8gOs_ldXFk

38   http://www.nbcnews.com/id/17388372/ns/politics-decision_08/t/
reading-hillary-rodhams-hidden-thesis/#.U8gOs_ldXFk

39   http://www.nbcnews.com/id/17388372/ns/politics-decision_08/t/
reading-hillary-rodhams-hidden-thesis/#.U8gOs_ldXFk

40   D'Souza 77.

41   D'Souza 59.

42   http://eaglerising.com/8728/obamas-terrible-legacy-set/

43   D'Souza 85.

44   Alinsky, Saul, *Rules for Radicals: A Pragmatic Primer for Realistic Radicals*,
USA: Vintage Books Edition, 1989.

45   Alinsky, Saul D., *Reveille for Radicals*, New York, Random House, 1946.

46   http://www.intercollegiatereview.com/index.php/2014/05/19/why-
academic-freedom-matters-now-more-than-ever/

47   http://en.wikipedia.org/wiki/Political_correctness

48   http://www.merriam-webster.com/dictionary/politically%20correct

49   http://www.webster-dictionary.org/definition/political%20correctness

50   http://m.washingtonpost.com/opinions/george-f-will-the-government-decided-that-redskins-bothers-you/2014/06/27/669558a6-fd54-11e3-932c-0a55b81f48ce_story.html

51   https://www.bing.com/search?q=ideology+definition&qs=AS&sk=HS 1&pq=ideology&sc=8-8&sp=2&cvid=45d32f061e22455783b71993c5648a93& FORM=QBLH

52   CollegeCalc (/) tallies the total costs for one academic year at Rutgers is in excess of 26K for New Jersey residents and nearly 40K for out of state residents.

53   http://articles.philly.com/2014-05-18/news/49928236_1_birgeneau-haverford-students-haverford-college

54   http://articles.philly.com/2014-05-18/news/49928236_1_birgeneau-haverford-students-haverford-college

55   CollegeCalc(/) states that one academic year at Haverford cost is in excess of a stunning $58K. If you want, your child and his or her radical friends to rule the roost while at college then break open the piggy bank and fork over 58K a year.

56   http://www.intercollegiatereview.com/index.php/2014/05/19/why-academic-freedom-matters-now-more-than-ever/

57   http://www.intercollegiatereview.com/index.php/2014/05/19/why-academic-freedom-matters-now-more-than-ever/

58   http://www.foxnews.com/us/2014/05/20/school-cancels-honors-night-for-being-too-exclusive/

59   http://www.washingtontimes.com/news/2014/may/20/ri-middle-school-cancels-honors-event-due-exclusiv/

60   http://www.washingtontimes.com/news/2014/may/20/ri-middle-school-cancels-honors-event-due-exclusiv/

61   Colson, Charles, *God & Government,* Grand Rapids, Michigan Zondervan, 2007, Pg. 237.

62   http://www.prisonplanet.com/texas-public-school-curriculum-teaches-students-to-design-a-socialist-flag-and-that-christianity-is-a-cult.html

63   http://www.prisonplanet.com/texas-public-school-curriculum-teaches-students-to-design-a-socialist-flag-and-that-christianity-is-a-cult.html

64   Shaver, Mathew D., *Faith and Freedom; A Complete Handbook for Defending Your Religious Rights, second edition,* Orlando, Florida, Liberty Counsel, 1998, Pg. 30,31.

65   Shaver 73.

66   http://www.theblaze.com/stories/2014/05/11/eleanor-clifts-absolutely-stunning-benghazi-claims-could-raise-your-blood-pressure-just-a-tad/

67   http://www.washingtonpost.com/sf/national/2014/05/30/how-the-va-developed-its-culture-of-coverups/

68   http://humanevents.com/2011/07/26/nasas-new-mission-boost-the-muslim-worlds-selfesteem/

69   http://www.foxnews.com/politics/2010/07/06/nasa-official-walks-claim-muslim-outreach-foremost-mission/

70 http://radio.foxnews.com/toddstarnes/top-stories/professor-angry-over-packages-for-troops-calls-them-shameful.html

71 http://en.wikipedia.org/wiki/Conscription_in_the_United_States

72 http://www.breakpoint.org/bpcommentaries/entry/13/25291

73 http://www.thegatewaypundit.com/2014/06/us-marine-barred-from-wearing-uniform-at-graduation-is-killed-in-afghanistan/

74 http://dailycaller.com/2014/06/14/public-universities-around-the-country-give-special-cords-to-gay-graduates-for-being-gay/

75 http://www.khou.com/news/local/Man-says-apartment-complex-called-his-US-flag-a-threat-to-Muslim-community-263757051.html

76 http://www.bizpacreview.com/2014/06/01/pows-dad-praises-allah-at-suspicious-rose-garden-press-conference-with-obama-122631

77 http://www.nydailynews.com/news/national/mom-be-headed-journalist-james-foley-knocks-obama-administration-article-1.1937114#ixzz3DDng5YWG

78 http://www.onebigdog.net/liberals-backtrack-on-wmd-and-war-pow-ers/

79 http://www.rushlimbaugh.com/daily/2014/06/18/these_are_great_times_for_barack_obama

80 http://www.weeklystandard.com/blogs/kerry-im-working-hard-have-lesbian-bisexual-and-transgender-ambassadors_795488.html

81 http://www.weeklystandard.com/blogs/kerry-im-working-hard-have-lesbian-bisexual-and-transgender-ambassadors_795488.html

82 http://en.wikipedia.org/wiki/LGBT_demographics_of_the_United_States

83 http://www.weeklystandard.com/blogs/kerry-im-working-hard-have-lesbian-bisexual-and-transgender-ambassadors_795488.html

84 http://www.ijreview.com/2014/06/148387-michelle-obama-neatly-summarizes-entire-progressive-agenda-nutrition-interview/

85 http://nypost.com/2014/05/22/nyc-says-this-girl-is-fat/

86 http://nypost.com/2014/05/22/nyc-says-this-girl-is-fat/

87 http://nypost.com/2014/05/22/nyc-says-this-girl-is-fat/

88 http://nypost.com/2014/05/22/nyc-says-this-girl-is-fat/

89 Forbes, Steve & Ames, Elizabeth, *Money: How the Destruction of the Dollar, Threatens the Global Economy – and What We Can Do About It*, McGraw-Hill, 2014. Pg.53.

90 D'Souza 226.

91 Hirschman, Albert O, *The Passion and the Interests; Political Arguments for Capitalism before Its Triumph*, Princeton, New Jersey, Princeton University Press, 1977. Pg. 9.

92 http://www.vision.org/visionmedia/biography-adam-smith/868.aspx

93 http://www.vision.org/visionmedia/biography-adam-smith/868.aspx

94   Hirschman 26.

95   Hirschman 28.

96   Forbes 55.

97   Hirschman 61.

98   Hirschman 80.

99   http://dictionary.reference.com/browse/free+markethttp://dictionary.reference.com/browse/free+market

100   http://www.economywatch.com/market-economy/us-market-economy.html

101   Forbes 41.

102   Hirschman 112.

103   http://www.huffingtonpost.com/miles-mogulescu/obamacares-flaws-put-prog_b_4310434.html'

104   http://mises.org/daily/4599

105   http://www.economywatch.com/market-economy/us-market-economy.html

106   http://www.economywatch.com/market-economy/us-market-economy.html

107   http://en.wikipedia.org/wiki/Innovation

108   D'Souza 158.

109   D'Souza 181.

110   D'Souza 181.

111   http://www.foxnews.com/politics/2014/05/22/house-committee-approves-bill-that-would-end-door-to-door-mail-for-15-million/

112   http://lastresistance.com/5920/louisiana-legislators-vote-exempt-gun-ban/#qtqQ0UtikbJWUrYs.99

113   http://www.ijreview.com/2014/05/141461-rules-needs-em-federal-judge-allowing-longtime-rep-run-despite-lacking-required-signatures/

114   Alcorn, Randy, Angela and Karina, *The Ishbane Conspiracy*, Sisters, Oregon, Multnomah Publishers, 2001. Pg. 145.

115   http://workplace.dispatch.com/content/stories/business/2014/03/30/eager-to-work-but-on-their-terms.htm

116   http://mic.com/articles/90111/if-you-re-under-30-you-re-much-more-interested-in-a-40k-job-than-a-100k-job

117   http://mic.com/articles/90111/if-you-re-under-30-you-re-much-more-interested-in-a-40k-job-than-a-100k-job

118   http://www.nydailynews.com/news/politics/39-millennials-vote-clinton-2016-poll-article-1.1861687#ixzz3AxSpIbOP

119   http://www.merriam-webster.com/dictionary/laissez-faire

120   D'Souza 223.

121 Forbes 49.

122 Forbes 50.

123 Forbes 9.

124 Forbes 9/10.

125 Gilder, George, *Knowledge and Power: The Information Theory of Capitalism and How it is Revolutionizing our World*, Washington, D.C.: Regnery Publishing, Inc., 2013. Pg. 123.

126 Forbes 11.

127 Forbes 80.

128 Forbes 81.

129 Forbes 18.

130 Forbes 17.

131 D'Souza 226.

132 Forbes 82.

133 http://www.huffingtonpost.com/mike-lux/obama-and-the-progressive_b_171083.html

134 http://www.huffingtonpost.com/mike-lux/obama-and-the-progressive_b_171083.html

135   http://money.cnn.com/2014/06/04/news/economy/american-dream/
index.html

136   Forbes 97.

137   Fergusson, Adam, *When Money Dies; The Nightmare of Deficit Spending,
Devaluation, and Hyperinflation in Weimar Germany,* New York, PublicAffairs, 2010.
Pg. viii.

138   Fergusson viii.

139   Fergusson 77.

140   Fergusson 117.

141   Fergusson 149.

142   Fergusson 157.

143   Fergusson 167.

144   Fergusson 201.

145   Fergusson 216.

146   Fergusson 223.

147   Fergusson 256.

148   Fergusson 254.

149   Fergusson 248.

150 Forbes 98.

151 Forbes 108.

152 Forbes 111.

153 Forbes 119.

154 Gilder 4.

155 Gilder 32.

156 Gilder 45.

157 Gilder 76.

158 Gilder 223.

159 Gilder 224.

160 Gilder 94.

161 Gilder 191.

162 Gilder 192.

163 http://politicaloutcast.com/2014/05/father-convicted-punished-mak-ing-son-walk-mile-home-school/#Pmh39KgGiuhvL57c.99

164 http://politicaloutcast.com/2014/05/father-convicted-punished-mak-ing-son-walk-mile-home-school/#Pmh39KgGiuhvL57c.99

165 http://www.foxbusiness.com/on-air/stossel/blog/2012/02/23/i-tried-open-lemonade-stand-illegal-everything-airs-tonight-9pm-fox-news-channel

166 http://www.foxbusiness.com/on-air/stossel/blog/2012/02/23/i-tried-open-lemonade-stand-illegal-everything-airs-tonight-9pm-fox-news-channel

167 http://www.stltoday.com/news/local/metro/hazelwood-girl-scout-cookie-case-could-be-shelved-as-lawyer/article_6100767a-f11f-11e1-ae99-001a4bcf6878.html#.U4-E4NO6ngo.gmail

168 http://www.foxbusiness.com/on-air/stossel/blog/2012/02/23/i-tried-open-lemonade-stand-illegal-everything-airs-tonight-9pm-fox-news-channel

169 http://www.foxbusiness.com/on-air/stossel/blog/2012/02/23/i-tried-open-lemonade-stand-illegal-everything-airs-tonight-9pm-fox-news-channel

170 http://oneduffy.blogspot.com/2014/06/i-am-mom.html

171 http://oneduffy.blogspot.com/2014/06/i-am-mom.html

172 http://www.arlnow.com/2014/05/02/new-regulations-ban-car-wash-fundraisers/

173 http://www.arlnow.com/2014/05/02/new-regulations-ban-car-wash-fundraisers/

174 http://www.examiner.com/article/what-life-socialist-europe-is-actually-like

175 http://worldtruth.tv/collecting-rainwater-now-illegal-in-many-states-as-big-government-claims-ownership-over-our-water/

176   http://www.ijreview.com/2014/06/143479-obama-unilaterally-impose-new-carbon-emission-caps-americas-power-plants/

177   http://aattp.org/33-u-s-cities-ban-sharing-food-with-the-homeless/

178   http://ncrenegade.com/editorial/town-bans-acts-of-charity-because-it-undercuts-need-for-government-agencies/

179   http://www.prisonplanet.com/arizona-student-suspended-for-having-gun-screen-saver.html

180   http://www.huffingtonpost.com/2013/06/11/pop-tart-gun_n_3419815.html

181   http://www.nydailynews.com/news/national/pennsylvania-5-year-old-suspended-bubble-gun-terrorist-threat-article-1.1243635#ixzz3AyBShS4u

182   http://www.foxnews.com/us/2013/01/29/massachusetts-boy-5-warned-by-school-for-making-lego-toy-gun/

183   http://www.guns.com/2013/06/04/students-suspended-for-nerf-guns-at-school/

184   http://www.nydailynews.com/news/national/va-7-year-old-suspended-gun-play-article-1.1337342

185   http://www.foxnews.com/us/2013/01/16/two-maryland-school-children-suspended-for-making-gun-gestures-with-hands/

186   http://en.wikipedia.org/wiki/Internal_Revenue_Service

187   Forbes 62.

188   Forbes 63.

189   Forbes 65.

190   Forbes 67.

191   Forbes 67.

192   Forbes 68.

193   Forbes 71.

194   Clairmont, Patsy, Graham, Mary, Johnson, Barbara, Johnson, Nicole, Meberg, Marilyn, Swindoll, Luci, Walsh, Sheila, Wells, Thelma, *Contagious Joy; Joyful Devotions to Lift Your Spirits*, Nashville, Tenn, W. Publishing Group, 2006. Pg. 122.

195   .facebook_1409534226604

196   http://wc.arizona.edu/papers/90/33/04_1_m.html

197   Gay Lesbian Straight Education Network

198   http://www.massresistance.org/docs/gen2/14b/GLSEN-Conference-040514/index.html

199   http://news.yahoo.com/atheist-mega-churches-root-across-us-world-214619648.html

200   Perry, James, Trending Toward Cultural Captivity-Learning to Survive the Inevitable. Chipley, Florida, Theocentric Publishers, Pg. 41,

201   http://www.americanthinker.com/2009/03/us_public_schools_teaching_chi_1.html

202   http://www.pbs.org/wgbh/pages/frontline/oj/view/

203   http://www.foxnews.com/entertainment/2014/09/17/joan-rivers-doctor-took-selfie-while-was-under-anesthesia-report-claims/

204   http://www.addictinginfo.org/2014/06/07/billionaire-gets-off/

205   http://www.huffingtonpost.com/2013/12/12/affluenza-defense-probation-for-deadly-dwi_n_4430807.html

206   http://www.humanevents.com/2012/03/22/sandra-fluke-admits-she-doesnt-know-what-birth-control-costs/

207   http://www.humanevents.com/2012/03/22/sandra-fluke-admits-she-doesnt-know-what-birth-control-costs/

208   http://www.jewsnews.co.il/2014/05/15/sandra-fluke-id-rather-be-a-captive-nigerian-girl-than-touched-by-a-republican/

209   http://www.lifenews.com/2014/05/14/former-abortion-clinic-owner-we-pushed-sex-ed-to-create-a-market-for-abortion/?utm_content=bufferfbceb&utm_medium=social&utm_source=twitter.com&utm_campaign=buffer

210   http://www.breakpoint.org/bpcommentaries/entry/13/25232

211   http://www.newsmax.com/US/abortion-video-YouTube-Emily-Letts/2014/05/07/id/569999/

212   http://catholicnewslive.com/story/114201

213   http://www.ijreview.com/2014/05/142528-gwyneth-paltrow-says-reading-mean-comments-online-like-surviving-war/

214   http://www.celebritynetworth.com/richest-celebrities/actors/gwyneth-paltrow-net-worth/

215   http://www.ijreview.com/2014/05/142632-green-beret-choice-words-gwyneth-paltrows-comparison-tweets-war/

216   http://www.channel933.com/onair/nathan-fast-50264/a-soldier-asked-eminem-for-an-12431039/#ixzz35CyKcT35

217   http://www.celebritynetworth.com/dl/eminem-salary/

218   http://drrichswier.com/2014/05/24/america-godless-army/

219   http://www.campusreform.org/?ID=5685

220   http://www.campusreform.org/?ID=5685

221   http://radio.foxnews.com/toddstarnes/top-stories/art-professor-student-defend-cross-vandalism.html

222   http://www.dailymail.co.uk/news/article-1142967/School-receptionist-faces-sack-year-old-daughter-told-talking-God.html

223   http://www.lifesitenews.com/news/catholic-couple-fined-13000-for-refusing-to-host-same-sex-wedding-at-their

224   http://www.foxnews.com/opinion/2014/08/20/student-punished-for-saying-bless/

225   http://www.u-s-history.com/pages/h1061.html

226   http://www.christianpost.com/news/how-liberalism-violates-all-10-commandments-119971/

227   https://www.biblegateway.com/passage/?search=Galatians+6%3A7&
version=NIV

228   Alcorn, Randy, *The Treasure Principle-Unlocking the Secret of Joyful Giving*,
Colorado Springs, Co. Multnomah Books, 2001. Pg. 52.

229   http://www.breakpoint.org/bpcommentaries/entry/13/25257

230   Limbaugh, David *Persecution: How Liberals are Waging a War on Christianity*, New York: Regnery Publishing, 2003. Pg. 300.

231   http://www.biblicalchristianworldview.net/documents/quotesRonal-
dReagan.pdf

232   http://www.breakpoint.org/bpcommentaries/breakpoint-commen-
taries-archive/entry/13/25335

233   http://www.breakpoint.org/bpcommentaries/breakpoint-commen-
taries-archive/entry/13/25335

234   http://finance.yahoo.com/blogs/daily-ticker/obama-s-new-student-
debt-plan-may-end-up-backfiring--aaron-task-141342087.html

235   Shaver, Mathew D., *Faith and Freedom; A Complete Handbook for Defending Your Religious Rights, second edition*, Orlando, Florida, Liberty Counsel, 1998,
Pg. 106.

236   http://www.truthandaction.org/christian-baker-forced-make-cake-
gay-couples/

237   http://www.truthandaction.org/christian-baker-forced-make-cake-
gay-couples/

238 http://www.truthandaction.org/christian-baker-forced-make-cake-gay-couples/

239 http://www.christianpost.com/news/with-the-days-of-comfortable-acceptable-christianity-now-over-dont-be-ashamed-of-the-gospel-robert-p-george-encourages-119688/

240 http://www.christianpost.com/news/with-the-days-of-comfortable-acceptable-christianity-now-over-dont-be-ashamed-of-the-gospel-robert-p-george-encourages-119688/

241 http://www.thepublicdiscourse.com/2014/05/13182/

242 http://www.thepublicdiscourse.com/2014/05/13182/

243 http://www.thepublicdiscourse.com/2014/05/13182/

244 https://mail.google.com/mail/u/0/?shva=1&pli=1#label/BOOK/1462987791d4ff99

245 http://www.thepublicdiscourse.com/2014/05/13182/

246 http://independentfilmnewsandmedia.com/graphic-quotes-yolande-nikki-giovanni/

247 http://www.bizpacreview.com/2014/05/25/history-teacher-poses-for-yearbook-photo-in-hoodie-bag-of-skittles-121163

248 http://www.foxnews.com/us/2014/05/20/school-cancels-honors-night-for-being-too-exclusive/

249 http://www.washingtontimes.com/news/2014/may/20/ri-middle-school-cancels-honors-event-due-exclusiv/

250   http://www.washingtontimes.com/news/2014/may/20/ri-middle-school-cancels-honors-event-due-exclusiv/

251   http://www.jsonline.com/news/grades-b9996297z1-223933981.html

252   http://www.washingtonpost.com/wp-dyn/content/article/2010/11/13/AR2010111304100_2.html?sid=ST2010111400180

253   http://articles.sun-sentinel.com/2013-04-27/news/fl-editorial-zero-to-50-grades-dv-20130427_1_graduation-rates-wrong-message-school-board

254   http://www.komonews.com/news/local/Angry-mom-School-awards-ceremony-featured-swearing-sex-toys-261759461.html

255   http://www.worldmag.com/2014/05/flip_this_country

256   http://www.worldmag.com/2014/05/flip_this_country

257   http://www.climatedepot.com/2014/06/12/fired-for-diverging-on-climate-progressive-professors-fellowship-terminated-after-wsj-oped-calling-global-warming-unproved-science/

258   http://www.theblaze.com/stories/2014/08/01/do-nothing-congress-house-passed-more-than-350-bills-that-sit-on-harry-reids-desk-says-congress-woman/#

259   http://www.urbandictionary.com/define.php?term=Ineptocracy&def id=6169496

260   http://pinstripepulpit.com/being-a-man-of-conviction-eric-metaxass-7-men/

261 http://m.christianpost.com/news/with-the-days-of-comfortable-acceptable-christianity-now-over-dont-be-ashamed-of-the-gospel-robert-p-george-encourages--119688/

262 http://www.churchleadership.org/apps/articles/default.asp?articleid=42346&columnid=4545

263 http://www.churchleadership.org/apps/articles/default.asp?articleid=42346&columnid=4545

264 http://www.pastorburnout.com/pastor-burnout-statistics.html

265 http://en.wikipedia.org/wiki/Mayflower_Compact

266 2nd Corinthians 2:11

267 http://en.wikipedia.org/wiki/Rules_for_Radicals

268 http://en.wikipedia.org/wiki/Saul_Alinsky

269 http://www.nationalreview.com/articles/294454/still-alinsky-play-book-john-fund

270 http://www.hillaryclintonquarterly.com/documents/HillaryClinton-Thesis.pdf

271 Alinsky, Saul, *Rules for Radicals: A Pragmatic Primer for Realistic Radicals*, USA: Vintage Books Edition, 1989. Pg. see above

272 http://en.wikipedia.org/wiki/Rules_for_Radicals

273 Alinsky, Saul, *Rules for Radicals: A Pragmatic Primer for Realistic Radicals*, USA: Vintage Books Edition, 1989. Pg. 126.

274

275   Alinsky, Saul, *Rules for Radicals: A Pragmatic Primer for Realistic Radicals*, USA: Vintage Books Edition, 1989.
Pg. 30.

276   Alinsky, Saul, *Rules for Radicals: A Pragmatic Primer for Realistic Radicals*, USA: Vintage Books Edition, 1989. Pg.30.

277   Alinsky, Saul, *Rules for Radicals: A Pragmatic Primer for Realistic Radicals*, USA: Vintage Books Edition, 1989. Pg. 130-131.

278   Alinsky, Saul, *Rules for Radicals: A Pragmatic Primer for Realistic Radicals*, USA: Vintage Books Edition, 1989. Pg. 154.

279   http://www.nationalreview.com/articles/294454/still-alinsky-play-book-john-fund/page/0/1

280   http://townhall.com/columnists/johnhawkins/2012/07/03/the_40_best_quotes_from_ronald_reagan/page/full

281   http://youthspecialities.com Youth Specialties Hot illustrations Volume 1.

282   http://www.brainyquote.com/quotes/quotes/e/edmundburk377528.html#C56sp8bY4rEbSoXV.99

283   http://www.answers.com/Q/What_is_the_origin_of_the_phrase_%27Evil_will_prevail_when_good_men_do_nothing%27

284   http://www.christianitytoday.com/ct/2007/october/36.156.html

285   Matthew 20:28 NIV

286   http://www.brainyquote.com/quotes/quotes/b/billygraha626304. html#LERyzOIKCiCifmak.99

287   http://billygraham.org/story/billy-graham-my-heart-aches-for-amer-ica/

288   http://christian-quotes.ochristian.com/christian-quotes_ochristian. cgi?find=Christian-quotes-by-Ronald+Reagan-on-America

289   http://youthspecialities.com Youth Specialties Hot illustrations Volume 1.

290   http://www.ijreview.com/2014/10/183137-facebook-post-baker-lost-shop-refusing-bake-lesbian-couples-cake-goes-viral/

291   http://www.americanthinker.com/blog/2014/09/dsouza_to_be_sent_to_reeducation_camp.html#ixzz3FCdqwawN

www.ingramcontent.com/pod-product-compliance
Lightning Source LLC
Chambersburg PA
CBHW070637290526
45790CB00001B/125